MONTESSORI'S CONCEPT OF PERSONALITY

Michael J. Gross

UNIVERSITY PRESS OF AMERICA

LANHAM • NEW YORK • LONDON

Copyright © 1978 by

University Press of America,® Inc.

4720 Boston Way
Lanham, MD 20706

3 Henrietta Street
London WC2E 8LU England

Library of Congress Cataloging in Publication Data

Gross, Michael J.
    Montessori's concept of personality.

    Bibliography: p.
    1. Montessori method of education.   2. Personality.
I. Title.
LB775.M8G67   1986   371.3'92   85-22530
ISBN 0-8191-5074-6 (alk. paper)
ISBN 0-8191-5075-4 (pbk. : alk. paper)

Second Printing, 1986

This book is dedicated to my grandfather

Ray C. Burke

who has been a source of encouragement,
inspiration, and wisdom for so many.

iii

The first duty of the educator, whether he is involved with the newborn infant or an older child, is to recognize the human personality of the young being and respect it.

Maria Montessori

The Child in the Church (1936)

PREFACE

A few years ago I was reading "Education and Peace" by Maria Montessori when I became intrigued by the repeated use of the word "personality." Then I selected other books by Montessori and noticed that she refers over and over again to the child's development of personality. Just what did she mean by "personality"? As with so many of the Montessori's works I thought that something may have been lost in the translation from Italian to English. Then I discovered Michael Gross' book, for which I am now writing the preface for the second edition.

Gross explains that Montessori's concept of personality is the total of the individual's potentiality. In a careful, methodical manner he analyzes many of Montessori's references to personality development and categorizes them according to physical and mental potentialities. As it is commonly used, personality is synonymous with idiosyncracy but in the Montessori context it is elevated to the status of positive attributes of growth. Montessori recognized that the "whole" human being was in-process and that an education based only on academic understanding was a mere portion of what is necessary. If we are to help young people develop so that they can take their place in society as fully integrated human beings, education has to consider all the factors that build the personality.

Gross' book is a major contribution to understanding the multi-dimensional characteristics of the Montessori concept of personality.

- Phil Gang
  Atlanta, Georgia

June, 1985

vi

TABLE OF CONTENTS

vii

INTRODUCTION

Maria Montessori was born of Alessandro and Renilde Montessori at Chiaraville, Italy, on August 31, 1870, and early in life displayed the courage and persistence that was later to give the world a new system of education. Her powerful inner determination to live out her life's mission and her ability to penetrate all male professions were evident as she enrolled, at the age of sixteen, in the previously masculine-dominated Michelangelo Buonarroti Technical School with the intention of becoming an engineer. Although she redirected her focus from engineering to medicine, her determination to succeed in a male-controlled profession was quite evident. Having been told by the head of the Board of Education in Rome that she could not enter the University as a student in medicine, Montessori stated quite frankly while shaking hands, "I shall study medicine,"[1] and on July 10, 1896, Maria Montessori was awarded a doctor's diploma in medicine and surgery by the Royal University of Rome.

During her first two years of hospital work (1896-1898) Montessori nurtured a special interest in children with "nervous and mental diseases." Her curiosity to find appropriate methods for helping these children led Montessori to the Bourneville institute in Paris, where she studied the educational works of Jean Itard and Edward Seguin.

In 1898 she was appointed director of the Orthophrenic Institute in Rome, which was created to prepare special teachers to aid in the education of the mentally handicapped. From the beginning of her work with these children Montessori considered her methods not limited particularly to the instruction of the mentally regarded.

> I believe that they contained
> educational principles more
> rational than those in use; so
> much so, indeed, that through their
> means an inferior mentality would
> be able to grow and develop.
> This feeling, so deep as to be
> in the nature of an intuition,
> became my controlling idea and

> after I had left the school
> for deficients, and, little by
> little, I became convinced that
> similar methods applied to normal
> children would develop or set free
> their personality in a marvelous and
> surprising way.[2]

This controlling idea led Montessori to register as a student of philosophy at University of Rome, engaging in the study of normal pedagogy and the principles upon which it is based."[3] Concurrently with these studies, she lectured on anthropology and hygiene at the Royal Feminine Teacher Training College (1900-1904). In 1904 she was appointed lecturer of anthropology at the University of Rome. Her work with deficient children, her study of the educational works of Itard and Seguin, and her study of "normal pedagogy" fostered the belief that her methods would be applicable to the education of normal children. It was this belief that served as the impetus for what was to become known as the Montessori method. It was not until 1906 that she was able to put her ideas into practice and thereby to further develop her method.

Edouardo Talamo, the director general of the Roman Association for Good Building, invited Montessori to establish "infant schools in its model tenements." Because she saw this as an opportunity not only to help young children but also to implement and test the ideas which had occupied her thinking for so many years, on January 6, 1907, Montessori formally opened her first Casa dei Bambini in the San Lorenzo district in Rome. It was there that she further developed the Montessori method. Other children's Houses were founded in the city of Rome and subsequently throughout the world.

From 1907 until her death May 6, 1952, in Holland, Montessori labored on behalf of the young child. She lectured, provided training courses, founded schools; and while her focus was on the young child, her vision included the whole of humanity.

Montessori's breadth of knowledge provided by her study of anthropology, philosophy, and psychology was complemented by a specialization in the sciences. Thus, her preparation was particularly appropriate for a half-century of dedicated service to the young child and ultimately to the cause of world peace. She delivered lectures on peace in Geneva, Brussels, and Copenhagen under the auspices of the Utrecht Scientific Society and before the organization of the World Fellowship of Faiths. Her candidacy for the

Nobel Peace Prize in 1949, 1950, and 1951 gives testimony to her labors on behalf of world peace. She had earlier been awarded an honorary Doctorate of Letters by the University of Durham on December 11, 1923. From the educational Institute of Scotland in Edinburgh she received the degree of Honorary Fellow on November 9, 1946.

The Association Montessori Internationale (AMI), founded in Denmark in 1929, has generated National Montessori Societies in over ten countries. The AMI headquarters in Denmark oversees training centers in numerous countries in America, Europe, Africa, and Asia. The Montessori method has become an integral part of American education since its reintroduction to the United States by Nancy McCormick Rambusch in the late 1950's, and presently there are schools and training careers affiliated with both the Montessori Association Internationale (AMI) and the American Montessori Association (AMS).

The Montessori method of education was developed from and is consistent with its author's concept of personality and its natural pattern of development. Montessori's scientific observation of children disclosed the natural process by which a child's personality is organized. With this natural growth pattern in mind Montessori developed a sequence of didactic materials which would assist and safeguard personality development. While her didactic materials received most of the attention, Montessori labored to point out that the human personality should be the focal point. She clarifies this point in the following passage:

> One would like to know in a few clear words what this Montessori method really is. We must consider the human personality and not a method of education. For the word "method" we should substitute something like this: "Help given in order that the human personality may achieve its independence," or "means offered to deliver the human personality from the oppression of age-old prejudices regarding education."[4]

Clearly, Montessori's focus is on the human personality. The present treatise is an attempt to organize and to clarify her central concept of personality and in this way to render her method easier to understand and practice.

The study will be divided into four chapters. Chapter I will define Montessori's CONCEPT OF PERSONALITY as the totality of an

individual's potentiality. Chapter II will
define Montessori's CONCEPT OF CHARACTER as
the healthy organization of personality.
Chapter III will define her CONCEPT OF
EDUCATION and discuss its relation to the
development of personality and to the
formation of character. Chapter IV will
first summarize the concept of personality
and the related concepts of character and
education and will then discuss William Heard
Kilpatrick's criticism of the Montessori
System and David Norbert Campbell's analysis
of that criticism.

CHAPTER I

MONTESSORI'S CONCEPT OF PERSONALITY

PERSONALITY, according to Montessori, is the totality of an individual's potentiality, since the aim of education is the development of the whole personality--that is, the development of all the mental and physical potencies--the purpose of the Montessori method of education is to aid in the development and harmonization of the whole personality. Montessori defines both the objective of her method and the nature of personality in this statement from The Child in the Church:

> . . . its object is to influence
> the whole life of the child: it
> aims, in short, at a total
> development of the personality,
> a harmonious growth of all the
> potentialities of the child,
> mental and physical, according
> to the laws of its being.[5]

While Montessori delineates the CONCEPT OF PERSONALITY according to MENTAL and

PHYSICAL powers, her references to personality are not always in terms of mental and physical capacities. Additional sets of terminology have been used by Montessori with regard to personality. This chapter will delineate Montessori's concepts of personality according to the mental and physical categories. Additional sets of terminology used by Montessori will likewise be presented and discussed.

The development of all potentialities and their harmonious interaction result in and are expressed by MOVEMENT. Movement, physical activity, or behavior is the expression of personality, and behavior that expresses a healthy personality is termed CHARACTER. Conversely, a lack of harmony among the various potentialities results in aimless or less-healthy behavior; that is, behavior exhibiting "defects in character," or a "lack of character." Movement, therefore, is a behavioral expression of the degree to which the mental and physical potentialities have developed and harmonized. The movement of a newborn child manifests a low level of development, since the physical abilities of the infant are not yet coordinated with his mental powers. In the course of development, the physical and mental abilities grow and coalesce, and the result is movement in a more perfect form. These increasingly higher levels of one's behavior manifest progression in the growth and organization of one's personality. Therefore, a healthy organization of personality reflects a rise from the vegetative level of activity to a higher and more comprehensive spiritual plane. Montessori discusses the need for healthy interaction between the mental and physical potentialities and their relation to movement in these statements from Absorbent Mind:

> Let us review man's nervous sys-
> tem in all its amazing complexity.
> In the first place, we have the
> brain (or "center"). Then there
> are the various sense organs, which
> collect impressions and pass them
> on to the brain. Thirdly, there
> are the muscles. And nerves, what
> do they do? These are like cables
> for transmitting nervous energy to
> the muscles. And this energy is
> what controls the movements of the
> muscles. So the organization has
> three main parts, brain, senses and
> muscles. Movement is the final
> result to which the working of all
> these delicate mechanisms lead up.
> In fact, it is only by movement
> that the personality can express
> itself.[6]

Coordinated movement, then, is the result of, and is dependent upon, the harmonious interaction of the nervous system, sense organs, and muscles. The "center" of the nervous system, the brain, must fuse with the other two factors: "If we have a brain, sense organs and muscles, all these must cooperate."[7]

In the following passage from The Secret of Childhood, Montessori explains that the integration of the elements of personality is brought about through the interaction of the SPIRITUAL EMBRYO (that is, the individual with all his latent potentialities) and his environment. More precisely, she maintains that the development and organization of the elements of personality are "occasioned" by the environment, while the satisfaction of an impulse is more directly the "cause" of development. Moreover, the less chaotic and more directed and perfected the movements, the more they reflect the increasingly integrated personality.

> There is an interchange between the individual, the spiritual embryo, and its environment. It is through the environment that the individual is molded and brought to perfection. A child is forced to come to terms with his surroundings and the efforts entailed lead to an integration of his personality. This slow and gradual activity brings about a continuous conquest of the instrument by the spirit

which must keep vigilant watch over
its sovereignty so that its motions
do not die from inertia or become
mechanical. The spirit must be in
constant command so that movements
which are not under the direction
of fixed instincts do not
degenerate into chaos. The effort
required to prevent this builds up
its energies and contributes to the
unending work of spiritual
incarnation. In this way, just as
the embryo becomes a child and a
child becomes a man, so the human
personality is formed through its
own efforts.[8]

With this general introduction to the
relation of behavior and personality (that
is, the relation of movement and one's
various potentialities) a closer analysis of
the concept of personality may begin.

As has been noted, Montessori equates
one's PERSONALITY with the totality of his
MENTAL and PHYSICAL potentialities, and
regards its development as synonymous with
the harmonious integration of these various
abilities. Montessori succinctly outlines
this conception of personality in the
statement that the aim of her method is a
"total development of the personality, a
harmonious growth of all the potentialities
of the child, physical and mental, according
to the laws of its being."[9]

Her categorization of potentialities in

terms of physical and mental factors is her
most consistent and understandable one. In
Education and Peace she describes the total
personality in terms of these physical and
mental capabilities:

> The human personality must be
> given a chance to realize every one
> of its capabilities. Men today are
> forced to take up either a trade or
> a profession. We might say that
> those who work only with their
> minds are mutilated men and those
> who work with their hands are de-
> capitated men. We try to create
> a harmony between those who work
> with their minds and those who
> work with their hands by appealing
> to their sentiments, but there
> is a need for whole men. Every
> side of the human personality
> must function.[10]

Montessori's   detailed   discussion   of
child-development   processes   throughout
Absorbent   Mind   reveals   clearly   the
classification of potentialities according to
physical and mental factors. Her balanced
emphasis   on   both   the   biological   and
psychological maturation seems to correspond
to her physical vs. mental bifurcation.

> As I have so often said, it is true
> that we cannot make a genius. We
> can only give to each individual
> the chance to fulfill his potential
> possibilities. But if we are to
> speak of a process of "biological
> maturation," we must also be

prepared to recognize a process of
"psychological maturation."[11]

What specifically does Montessori mean by the
term PHYSICAL FACTORS?

She identifies two "arrangements of the
human body": the SYSTEM OF RELATIONSHIPS and
the VEGETATIVE SYSTEM. The system of
relationship, or the voluntary nervous
system, includes the brain, sense organs, and
muscles. The vegetative system, or autonomic
system, refers to the involuntary, reflexive
functioning of the body.

> Physiologists regard the muscles as
> a part of the central nervous
> system, saying that this works as a
> whole to put man in relationship
> with his surroundings. In fact
> this whole apparatus of brain,
> senses and muscles, is often called
> the system of relationship, meaning
> that it puts man into touch with
> his world, living and nonliving,
> and therefore with other people.
> Without its help a man could have
> no contact with his surroundings or
> his fellows. Compared with this,
> all the other arrangements of the
> human body are--so to
> speak--selfish, because they serve
> only the person himself. They
> enable him to keep alive, or (as we
> say) to "vegetate," and therefore
> they are called "organs and systems
> of the vegetative life." The
> vegetative systems only help their
> owner to grow and exist. It is the
> system of relationship which puts

him into contact with the world.
The vegetative system provides for
a man's physical well-being and
enables him to enjoy the best of
health. But we have to think quite
differently about the nervous
system. This gives us the beauty
of our impressions, the perfections
of our thought. It is the source
of all inspiration. So it is wrong
for it to be lowered to the
vegetative level.[12]

Montessori intends the PHYSICAL potentialities of personality to refer to the SYSTEM OF RELATIONSHIPS; that is, the BRAIN, SENSE ORGANS, and MUSCLES. Unlike the vegetative functions, the brain, sense organs, and muscles have an obvious potency. The vegetative functions are not related to the mental personality in the same sense as are the brain, sense organs, and muscles. The VEGETATIVE LIFE of the individual refers to the NORMAL FUNCTIONING of the body; that is to such activities as the assimilation of food, circulation of blood, and breathing. In contrast to the brain, sense organs, and muscles, the various vegetative functions, "although they are connected to the nervous system, are independent of the will."[13] The essential difference, therefore, between the vegetative life and the voluntary nervous system is the relationship with the will.

Thus-unlike the vegetative functions - the brain, sense organs, and muscles <u>are</u> related to the will. Furthermore, recalling the interactive nature of the physical and mental potentialities, one can accept as understandable that the physical potentialities are to include the brain, sense organs, and muscles and are to exclude the vegetative functions. For example, the sensory-motor organs are guided and directed by the intellectual and volitional capacities; whereas this type of relationship does not exist between the vegetative and mental functions.

The distinction therefore between the two levels of physical capacity is between the vegetative system and the system of relationships. Moreover, it is understandable and consistent to distinguish between the potentialities of the vegetative functions and those of the brain, sense organs, and muscles. The latter have the potential for development and functioning and are related to the will. In contrast, the vegetative functions are for the most part "constant" and "fixed." By PHYSICAL FACTORS OF PERSONALITY Montessori means, therefore, the potentialities of the BRAIN, SENSE ORGANS, and MUSCLES rather than the "constant" vegetative functions. This is not to say, however, that the latter do not influence the personality and ultimately its resultant physical activity. Certainly the vegetative functions can operate at different levels of efficiency, and these various levels would definitely influence one's physical activity, which is the expression of personality. The vegetative functions, although they do not influence personality in some sense, have not the same potency as the brain, sense organs, and muscles. Thus, the physical factors of personality are confined to the brain, sense organs, and muscles. These physical factors and their need to grow are indicated in a discussion of the development of the power to stand and walk:

> The power to stand upright and to walk on two legs only, requires a most elaborate nervous organization, composed of several parts. One of these is the cerebellum, or hindbrain, situated at the base of the brain itself. Exactly at the age of six months, the cerebellum begins to develop at great speed. It continues this rapid growth till the fourteenth or fifteenth month, and then its pace slows down, but it continues growing nonetheless till the child is four and a half. The power to stand up and walk depends on this development. It is easy to follow

in the child. In reality there are two developments which follow one another. The child at six months begins to sit up, and at nine to crawl, or slide himself along, on hands and feet. Then he stands at ten months and walks at twelve to thirteen months. By the fifteenth month he is sure on his legs. The other part of this complex process is in the completion of certain nerves. Unless the spinal nerves were complete, which convey orders to the muscles of the legs, these orders could not be delivered. The completion of these nerves, which takes place in this period, is necessary for the control of those muscles. Thus many elements of a complex piece of development have to be harmonized if walking is to be achieved. A third element is the development of the skeleton. As we have seen, the child's legs at birth are not completely ossified. They are partly cartilaginous, and therefore still soft. How could they support his body like that? The skeleton has to harden before the child begins walking.[14]

Although Montessori classified the brain among the physical potentialities because it is a physical organ which must develop and which has potentialities, its functions involve intellectual activity and are therefore categorized among the mental potentialities.

The MENTAL POTENTIALITIES of personality

are one's INTELLECTUAL, VOLITIONAL, AFFECTIVE and MORAL abilities. The INTELLECTUAL abilities discussed by Montessori are primarily those of distinguishing, classifying, and cataloging.

> To collect facts and distinguish between them is the initial process in intellectual construction.[15]

> To be able to distinguish, classify, and catalog external things on the basis of a secure order already established in the mind--this is at once intelligence and culture.[16]

That one's intellectual abilities are a part of one's mental potentialities is a straight forward and familiar concept. In the Absorbent Mind Montessori discusses the additional intellectual powers of "imagination and abstraction" by which one is able to think of things not immediately present.[17] Although Montessori considers the intellectual abilities separately, they are related to the volitional, affective, and moral forces, and eventually must harmonize with those of the physical realm.

The second ability of the mental category is VOLITIONAL ENERGY, which directs one's physical abilities. In other words, will power is that mental activity which gives direction to the "voluntary muscles."

According to Montessori, during the first year of life the infant's will is not functioning. Rather, nature's will "imposes" itself upon the newborn child and directs his interests and activities. As the infant's will develops and is coordinated with other mental potentialities, its volitional influence and control increase, and nature's influence diminishes. Moreover, since it is the intellectual, affective, and moral elements that provide information and criteria by which the child makes decisions, the quality of his choices must be contingent upon the influence of these elements. Moreover, such quality increases as his input expands in quantity and quality. Ideally, then, the guidance and direction supplied by volitional energy are refined in quality as they are influenced by intellectual, affective, and moral elements.

The earlier discussion of physical potentialities pointed out the necessity of an interaction between physical and mental factors, especially the volitional energy. The expression of this interaction is one's behavior or movement. According to Montessori, the infant's movements are first "controlled" or "directed" by an unconscious impulse. Given a suitable environment, this

"vital impulse (homme)" evolves into a
conscious activity of the will.

> That which at first was but a
> vital impulse (homme) has become
> a deliberate act. The little
> child's first movements were
> instinctive. Now, he acts
> consciously and voluntarily,
> and with this comes an awakening
> of his spirit.[18]

Montessori summarizes the "energy of
volition" as a factor of mental life and
clarifies its relation to the physical
abilities in the following statement from
Absorbent Mind:

> Now, the muscles directed by the
> brain are called voluntary muscles,
> meaning that they are under the
> control of the will, and will power
> is one of the highest expressions
> of the mind. Without the energy
> of volition, mental life could
> hardly be said to exist.[19]

Moreover, the interaction of one's will with
one's physical abilities results in and is
expressed by MOVEMENT. Montessori emphasizes
that the will is not simply an "impulse
towards movement," but rather, it is the
"intelligent direction of movements."

> The whole external expression of
> the will is contained in movement:
> whatever action man performs,
> whether he walks, works, speaks or
> writes, opens his eyes to look, or
> closes them to shut out a scene, he

acts by "motion." An act of the will may also be directed to the restriction of movement: to restrain the disorderly movements of anger; not to give way to the impulse which urges us to snatch a desirable object from the hand of another, are voluntary actions. Therefore, the will is not a simple impulse towards movement, but the intelligent direction of movements.[20]

The evolution from impulse activity to intelligently and morally guided activity corresponds to the construction and continued reconstruction of the will. One's ability to make decisions and to make them intelligently and morally is a matter of development. The child "constructs" his own will by a process of self-education. That is, the child develops his will by making decisions. His intellectual and moral elements act in a preparatory role in that they prepare him for making his own decisions. Montessori discusses the interaction of the mental and physical aspects involved in the development of one's will as follows:

Our little children are constructing their own wills when, by a process of self-education, they put in motion complex internal activities of comparison and judgment, and in this way make their intellectual acquisitions with order and clarity; this is a

kind of "knowledge" capable of
preparing children to form their
own decisions, and one which makes
them independent of the suggestions
of others; they can then decide in
every act of their daily life; they
decide to take or not to take; they
decide to accompany the rhythm of a
song with movement; they decide to
check every motor impulse when they
desire silence. The constant work
which builds up their personality
is all set in motion by decisions;
and this takes the place of the
primitive state of chaos, in which,
on the other hand, actions were the
outcome of impulses. A voluntary
life develops gradually within
them; and doubt and timidity
disappear, together with the
darkness of the primitive mental
confusion.[21]

Therefore, the second ability of the mental
potentialities, according to Montessori, is
volitional energy.

One's AFFECTIVE RESPONSE represents a
third category of mental potentialities.
This response is a mental force which
underlies the various factors of mental
personality and thereby influences the
physical factors.

According to Montessori, nature guides
an individual's development by means of
"primitive impulses" which, if satisfied by
suitable nourishment from the environment,
evoke feelings of joy and satisfaction. This

underlying positive, affective response accompanies those experiences conducive to the healthy development of the personality. Educational experiences, then, should correspond to the individual's "primitive impulse" in order that the coordination of impulse and appropriate stimuli may foster personality.

In contrast, feelings of uneasiness and incompleteness accompany experiences not conducive to healthy development. Since a positive, affective response accompanies healthy intellectual development as well as proper moral development, Montessori advises that the affective response must be the basis and foundation of intellectual and moral development and that, in the absence of such a foundation, the direction of one's development is questionable. A suitable environment, then, must "include a basis of feeling, and be built up thereupon, if we are not to lead the child towards illusion, falsity and darkness."[22]

Montessori maintains that one's emotional response, evoked by an activity conducive to development, is forever imprinted in the mind. Similarily, an emotional response accompanying activity unfavorable to development also remains with the child. Thus, Montessori states that "both the impressions the child's mind receives, and the emotional consequences they provoke, tend to remain permanently registered in it."[23]

Moral PERSONALITY is the term Montessori uses to indicate the fourth category of mental potentiality. Moral personality is that aspect which is involved with conscious decisions of right and wrong. The child in the first stage of development, ages zero to six, functions "outside the notions of morality." It is during the second period, ages six to twelve, that the child becomes conscious of right and wrong. "Problems of right and wrong are characteristic of this age; moral consciousness is being formed, and this leads later to the social sense."[24]

Montessori's discussion of morality focuses on two notions: first, a learned "pattern of behavior," and second, one's "moral conscience."

The concept of moral personality to which Montessori refers most often and with most clarity is the concept of a learned pattern of behavior. Implying her notion of the "absorbent mind" Montessori explains that the child simply "absorbs" a pattern of moral behavior. Just as the child "absorbs" language, so also does he "absorb" the moral habits of a people. It is during the creative period, zero to six, that the child assimilates "the customs, morals, and religion of a people."[25] This learned pattern of moral habits establishes guidelines for behavior and clarifies the distinction between what is good and what is evil; it therefore has a potential impact on the direction of one's choices. Like the other factors of the personality, the moral abilities must develop or solidify so as to promote the healthy development of the whole personality. Without such moral guidance one remains "unbalanced" or uncertain as to the proper course of action.

Montessori explains that this guidance-yielding pattern is "potent," "creative," and gives "form to the personality."[26] The moral capacity, especially in the sense of this first stage, influences the development and form of the total personality. But her second stage--moral conscience--introduces significant difficulties.

In one of only a few references to MORAL CONSCIENCE she differentiates between the absoluteness of the "voice of conscience" and the relativity of the "acquired social habits."

> It is possible that good and evil may be distinguished by means of an "internal sense," apart from cognitions of morality; and in such a case, of course, the good and evil in question would be absolute; that is to say, they would be bound up with life itself and not with acquired social habits. We always speak of a "voice of conscience" which teaches us from within to distinguish the two things: good confers serenity, which is order (and) enthusiasm, which is strength; evil is signalized as an anguish which is at times unbearable: remorse, which is not only darkness and disorder, but fever, malady of the soul.[27]

What is at issue here is the criterion for distinguishing between good and evil. In Montessori's first conception of morality the criterion is clearly a social one, and one that is relative to the behavioral patterns of a specific people. In contrast to this situational criterion is her second concept of an "internal sense," which is "bound up with life itself and not with acquired social habits." This second notion involves the dual aspects of "sensations" and "conditions suitable to life."

Both aspects of this second idea of morality, "sensations" and "conditions suitable to life," are criteria for distinguishing between good and evil. The first aspect involves a "sensation which warns us of perils, and causes us to recognize the circumstances favorable to life." Thus, the determining element is a feeling or sensation. Montessori has stated that good confers serenity and enthusiasm while evil evokes anguish and remorse.

The second aspect of this concept of morality concerns the "conditions favorable to life" as well as those which are obstacles to life. An internal sensation causes one to recognize the suitability of the circumstances. This emphasis on the conditions suitable to life underlies Montessori's view that this criterion is "bound up with life itself, and not with acquired social habits." Thus this second notion of moral personality, according to Montessori, involves an absoluteness not present in the first, but is the normal complement in the progression from the level of a learned pattern of behavior to the higher level involving an inner sense.

Montessori's writing indicate, therefore, that the mental potentialities can be categorized according to the interrelated intellectual, volitional, affective, and moral subfactors. These various components must develop and then cooperate with the physical potentialities. The expression of these interacting potentialities is physical activity, or in other words, behavior or movement. Moreover, according to Montessori's scheme, the harmonious organization of these potentialities is self-directed behavior, or character. In other words, character is the result of a healthy development of personality.

In summary, PERSONALITY is, according to Montessori, the totality of one's PHYSICAL and MENTAL POTENTIALITIES. The PHYSICAL factors have been identified as the anatomical members of the central nervous system: the BRAIN, SENSE ORGANS, and MUSCLES. The MENTAL factors are one's INTELLECTUAL, VOLITIONAL, AFFECTIVE, and MORAL abilities. Each of the physical and mental elements must first develop and then become coordinated. The role of the mental abilities in the guidance and control of the physical functions. This development and harmonious interaction of the two groups of elements finally result in the HEALTHY ORGANIZATION OF PERSONALITY: VIRTUOUS BEHAVIOR, or a MAN OF CHARACTER.

Throughout her writings Montessori has

employed additional statements in referring
to the various potentialities of personality.
These additional statements suggest that
Montessori was consistent in her general
outline insofar as the concept of personality
is concerned. At the same time they also
indicate that she did not adhere at all times
to one morphology of personality in all its
detail. The following four sets of
terminology will be considered in view of the
concept of personality as developed above:

    First: "Psychic energy and
               movement,"

    Second: "Sentiment and direction
               of ... ideation."

    Third: "Internal personality" and
               "inner personality," and

    Fourth: "Reflex personality."

First, Montessori describes "psychic
energy" and "movement" as two constituent
factors of personality. These two factors
must unify to avoid deviations in one's
personality development. Montessori
describes the necessity for psychic energy to
be united with movement in a Chapter on
"Deviation" in The Secret of Childhood:

    The concept of incarnation can thus
    be taken as a guide for
    interpreting deviant traits:
    psychic energy must be incarnated
    in movement so that it can unify

the personality of the agent. If this unity is not attained, either because of adult domination or lack of motivation for the child in his environment, the two constituent factors, psychic energy and movement, develop separately and "the man is divided." Since nothing is created or destroyed in nature, a child's psychic energies will either develop as they should or go off in wrong directions. Such deviations generally occur when these energies lose their finality and wander aimlessly about. The mind, which should be building itself up through voluntary, physical activities, then takes refuge in fantasies.[28]

Psychic energy is the combination of the mental potentialities interacting with the physical potentialities for the specific purpose of expressing itself in movement. If psychic energy is prevented from expressing itself, or if one's movement is not unified with psychic energy, the consequence is a deviation. Thus, the term psychic energy refers to both mental and physical elements, with movement, on the other hand, indicating the actual activity or behavior. Generally, the two terminologies so used are compatible with the mental and physical categorization of potentialities of personality. Still, to identify them as "two constituent factors" of personality may cause confusion; for movement is really the expression of personality, while psychic energy as has been stated is mental potentialities interacting with physical potentialities.

Secondly, in a discussion of the concept of "character" in Spontaneous Activity in Education, Montessori defines the whole personality in terms of "the sentiments of the individual and the direction of his ideation."

> There is a voluntary fundamental
> quality upon which not only are the
> superficial relations between man
> and man based, but on which the
> very edifice of society is erected.
> This quality is known as "continu-
> ity." The social structure is
> founded upon the fact that men can
> work steadily and produce within
> certain average limits on which the
> economic equilibrium of a people is
> constructed. The social relations
> which are the basis of the repro-
> duction of the species are founded
> upon the continuous union of
> parents in marriage. The family
> and productive work: these are the
> two pivots of society; they rest
> upon the great volitive quality;
> constancy, or persistence. This
> quality is really the exponent of
> the uninterrupted concord of the
> inner personality. Without it, a
> life would be a series of episodes,
> a chaos; it would be like a body
> disintegrated into its cells,
> rather than an organism which
> persists throughout the mutations

> of its own material. This funda-
> mental quality, when it embraces
> the sentiment of the individual and
> the direction of his ideation, that
> is to say, his whole personality,
> is what we have called character.
> The man of character is the persis-
> tent man, the man who is faithful
> to his own word, his own convic-
> tions, his own affections.[29]

In this contest, "sentiments of the individual" refers to an individual's feelings or attitudes; that is, to the affective element of mental personality. The "direction of his ideation" coincides with the intellectual element of mental personality. Together with constancy, which is will, the affective and the intellectual constitute the inner personality. When the inner personality exhibits an uninterrupted harmony, it displays the quality of "continuity." Continuity represents quality of behavior that is controlled by the will. Furthermore, this type of behavior results in character. Thus, when continuity "embraces" the affective and intellectual elements of personality, the result is character. This is to say, when the elements of personality have established a continuous interrelationship, the man of character, the persistent man, emerges.

Thirdly, how do the terms "inner personality" and "internal personality" fit into the mental/physical categorization? In a chapter titled "Intelligence" in Spontaneous Activity in Education, Montessori uses the terms inner and internal interchangeably:

> The child who is "free to move about," and who perfects himself by so doing, is he who has an "intelligent object" in his movements; the child who is free to develop his inner personality, who perseveres in a task for a considerable time, and organizes himself upon such a fundamental phenomenon, is sustained and guided by an intellectual purpose. Without this his persistence in work, his inner formation, and his progress would not be possible. When we refrain from guiding the subjugated child step by step, when, liberating the child from our personal influence, we place him in an environment suited to him and in contact with the means of development, we leave him confidently to "his own intelligence." His motor activity will then direct itself to definite actions: he will wash his hands and face, sweep the room, dust the furniture, change his clothes, spread the rugs, lay the table, cultivate plants, and take care of animals. He will choose the tasks conducive to his development and persist in material which leads him to distinguish one thing from another, to select, to reason, to correct himself; and the acquirements thus made are not only "a cause of internal growth" but a

strong propulsive force to further
progress. Thus, passing from
simple objects to objects of ever
increasing complexity, he becomes
possessed of a culture; moreover,
he organizes his character by means
of the internal order which forms
itself within him, and by the skill
which he acquires.[30]

Inner personality in this context
implies the intellectual, volitional, and
affective factors; that is, the mental
potentialities to the exclusion of the
physical factors. Throughout Montessori's
discussion of the development of the inner
personality she indicates the potentialities
involved. The child freely developing his
inner personality is he who is "sustained and
guided by an intelligent purpose."
Furthermore, he engages in activities "which
lead him to distinguish one thing from
another, to select, to reason, to correct
himself." Clearly, one's intellectual
potentialities are indicated by the term
inner personality. Secondly, the child
freely developing his inner personality is he
who "chooses the tasks conducive to his
development. Certainly one's volitional
energies are also indicated by the term inner
personality. Thirdly, choosing tasks
conducive to one's development produces the

affective responses of joy and satisfaction. Thus, one's affective energies are involved whenever there is a satisfaction or a frustration of one's inner urges.

As Montessori continues the consideration of intelligence, she substitutes "internal personality" for "inner personality." The "stable equilibrium in the internal personality which produces calm, strength, and the possibility of fresh conquests" refers to a coordination between the intellectual and volitional elements and a positive, affective response. Montessori uses "internal personality" synonymously with "inner personality"; and to identify INNER with MENTAL is compatible with her schema.

The final term needing clarification is reflex personality. Reflex personality refers, in general, to a basic assumption regarding the nature of personality. In Montessori's view, personality is "active" rather than "receptive"; it is responsive rather than passive. Reflex personality signifies specifically one's ability for psychical reflex activity. Montessori's single reference to "reflex personality" is in the following passage from Spontaneous Activity in Education:

Such an instrument may be compared

to a systematized "mental test."
It is not, however, established
upon a basis of external
measurement, for the purpose of
estimating the amount of
instantaneous psychical reaction
which it produces; it is, on the
contrary, a stimulus which is
itself determined by the psychical
reactions it is capable of
producing and maintaining
permanently. It is the psychical
reaction, therefore, that in this
case determines and establishes the
systematic "mental test." The
psychical reaction which
constitutes the sole basis of
comparison in the determination of
the tests, is a polarization of the
attention, and the repetition of
the actions related to it. When a
stimulus corresponds in this manner
to the "reflex personality," it
serves, not to measure but to
maintain a lively reaction; it is
therefore a stimulus to the
internal formation . . . .
Whereas the ancient pedagogy in all
its various interpretations started
from the conception of a "receptive
personality"--one, that is to say,
which was to receive instructions
and to be passively formed, this
scientific departure starts from
the conception of an active
personality--reflex and
associative--developing itself by a
series of reactions induced by
systematic stimuli which have been
determined by experiment.[31]

Unlike   such   terms   as   "inner
personality," "internal personality," and

"moral personality," which signify potentialities, "reflex personality" is used to describe an underlying assumption regarding the nature of personality. To replace the outdated concept of receptive personality, Montessori injects the notion of reflex personality. She believed the various potentialities developed in response to environmental stimuli rather than according to a more passive formula.

Reflex personality signifies specifically one's ability for psychical reflex activity. It signifies one's capability for "instantaneous psychical reaction." This reaction is a reflex response rather than a voluntary one. The psychic response is "a polarization of the attention, and the repetition of the actions related to it." Reflex personality involves, therefore, a psychical reflex activity; namely, an instantaneous psychical reaction induced by certain stimuli. Most crucial to Montessori's view is her use of this reflexive response to determine the suitability of a stimulus to foster growth.

When a stimulus activates the reflex personality, it serves "to maintain a lively reaction" and thereby to stimulate internal formation. In other words, when a stimulus results in concentration of attention and repetition of activity relative to the stimulus, it initiates organization of the personality and thereby reveals an appropriate didactic material.

Reflex personality denotes, therefore, the nature of personality as being active and response rather than passive. Moreover, it signifies specifically one's ability for instantaneous psychical activity. Montessori employs this reflex activity as an instrument in determining those stimuli which are suitable for one's development. This notion of reflex personality as describing personality's active nature seems consistent with the delineation of the concept as developed above. Moreover, reflex personality is compatible with the mental/physical categorization if one keeps in mind that the term refers to an underlying assumption rather than a category of potentialities.

CHAPTER 2

CHARACTER AS THE HEALTHY ORGANIZATION OF PERSONALITY

Montessori's concept of personality involves the total embodiment of one's mental and physical potentialities, the interrelation of which is expressed by movement; that is, by one's behavior. Behavior is not only the expression of this interrelation but also the result of the organization of the personality. In other words, the way in which the personality is organized is evidenced by the type of one's behavior.

An individual's behavior, then, reveals the manner in which the personality has been organized. The intent of this chapter is to present Montessori's notion that the healthy organization of personality yields a type of behavior designated by the term CHARACTER and in the course of discussion her references to to character will be listed and analyzed. The notion of CHARACTER as the behavioral traits of a well-organized personality will be presented as her most understandable and most consistent view of character. Furthermore, the role of "inner urges" will be be examined and discussed as Nature's mechanism for guiding the formation of character.

Behavior as the expression of personality can be viewed, generally speaking, as either normal or deviant. Does the term character cover both normal and deviant behaviors or just one, to the exclusion of the other? In this regard Montessori's use of the term is inconsistent. The following passages reveal that Montessori used the term character to refer sometimes to normal behavior and at other times to deviant behavior.

1) So, in this period, (0-2 years of age), we not only have the development of character to be normally expected, but certain malformations, or "deviations" of personality, may also be formed, which become serious at later stages of growth.[32]

2) Even in the face of the evidence that today there is an ever increasing number of problem children, backward children, children who lack in character and initiative, children with

a poor command of language who hesitate and stammer and grow up to be unbalanced, ...[33]

3) Children who have been prevented from developing fully often show character traits that disappear when they become normalized through work.[34]

4) Children of a weak and retiring character engage in similar activities, but their habits of accumulating things are regarded as perfectly normal.[35]

In statement (1) the "development of character" is distinguished from "deviation of personality." The distinction implies that the term for the healthy development of personality--that is, CHARACTER--does not include the "malformation or deviations" of personality; it includes only the traits of a well-developed personality. This meaning is consistent with Montessori's second statement that there is an "increasing number of problem children" who "lack in character and initiative." A person "lacking in character" is clearly lacking in virtuous traits. Thus, statements (1) and (2) show Montessori's use of the term character as meaning normal or virtuous behavioral traits only. Deviant traits are represented as a "lack of character." According to these statements, character denotes specifically and exclusively virtuous behavioral traits.

However, Montessori's use of this term is not always consistent with the above notion. She occasionally uses the term character to designate behaviors in general; that is, both virtuous and deviant behaviors. Statements (3) and (4) reveal her use of the term to indicate deviant as well as virtuous traits. In statement (3) the "character traits that disappear" are obviously deviant traits. Children whose potentialities have not fully developed exhibit deviant behavior, or deviant character traits, that will disappear when the child's potentialities meet with suitable conditions. Montessori's use of "weak and retiring character" in statement (4) reiterates this notion of character as encompassing both deviant and virtuous traits.

The inconsistency with which Montessori uses the term character can be displayed by a passage from Absorbent Mind, in which she first explains that character is developed as a result of environmental conditions. These conditions will either foster or frustrate growth. Thus, character is developed in a healthy manner by favorable conditions or in an unhealthy manner by unfavorable conditions. Character, then, would be regarded as healthy or unhealthy, virtuous or deviant, according to one's environment. However, several paragraphs later Montessori offers another explanation. She refers to the effects of an unsuitable environment and states that "we have a child devoid of character and unable to learn."[36] She is claiming that the child has not developed virtuous behavioral traits and thus lacks character. This latter reference to character as virtuous traits only is inconsistent with the more encompassing meaning she ascribes to it in her earlier paragraph.

While this discrepancy does at times cause some confusion, it does not substantially interrupt the concept of character and the relation of the latter to the concept of personality. Montessori's use of the term character indicates a reference to behaviors, but her most consistent use of the term denotes specifically and exclusively VIRTUOUS behavioral traits. Unlike personality, which signifies potentialities, character denotes the behaviors which result from potentialities. The following statements reveal the predominant reference to character as virtuous traits only.

> By character we mean the behavior of men driven (though often unconsciously) to make progress. This is the general tendency. Humanity and society have to progress in evolution.[37]

> The man of character is the persistent man, the man who is faithful to his own word, his own convictions, his own affections.[38]

The definition of character as "the behavior of men driven to make progress" suggests that the behavior referred to is exclusively virtuous behavior. More specifically, these virtuous traits are "persistency" and "faithfulness"; that is, constancy or continuity. The man of character is one whose behavior is constant; that is, one whose behavior reveals a stable organization of the elements of personality. Character is synonymous with those behaviors that result from a certain organization of the elements of personality and gives evidence of the harmonious relationship that exists among the elements of personality. The quality of one's behavior most revealing of such a relationship is that of "continuity." Thus, when "continuity embraces the sentiments of the individual and the direction of his ideation" the resulting behavior is termed character. Continuity is a fundamental quality of the type or organization of personality which in turn yields constant or persistent behavior. Character is, therefore, a term denoting the behavior of the "persistent man, the man who is faithful to his own word, his own convictions, and his own affections;"[39] and the man of character reveals a harmony among the elements of his personality, but also the resulting virtuous behavioral traits.

The elements of personality must develop and then harmonize with one another. At first they mature separately, but in the end must "become integrated" if the personality is to "construct itself normally." And a personality thus normally constructed results in virtuous behavioral traits, or character; while a personality which fails to unify its elements results in deviant behavior, or lack of character. From the perspective of behavior, one's virtuous traits--or one's character--indicate a normalized child; whereas deviant traits--or a lack of character--indicate an unhealthy organization of one's potentialities. Deviant behavior is, therefore, the result of conditions suitable to the development of personality. Montessori discusses the formation of character in terms of the development of personality in the following statement:

> It allows us to visualize the development of character as a natural sequence of events resulting from the child's own individual efforts, which have no reference to any extraneous factors, but depend on his vital creative energy, and on the obstacles he meets within daily life. Our interest is therefore turned towards the observation and interpretation of the work that nature does in the construction of man on his psychological side. We must do this from birth, when character and personality are zero, till the age in which they begin to disclose themselves. For, rooted in the unconscious mind, natural laws undoubtedly exist which determine psychological development and are common to all men. Differences, instead, depend largely on the vicissitudes of life: on the accidents, setbacks

and regressions produced in the
mental field by those obstacles
the obstacles the individual has
had to encounter in his path.[40]

Montessori emphasizes the natural course
of personality development; that is, its
course as guided by "natural laws." Quite
understandably, the task of the educator is
to determine the natural laws which guide the
growth of personality and consequently, the
formation of character. With this knowledge
he can provide suitable environmental
conditions which represent the "occasion" for
one's natural development. The formation of
character and the natural development of
personality require closer attention.
Specifically, certain of Montessori's
concepts--"incarnation," "spiritual embryo,"
"inner urges"--need to be analyzed.

Throughout Montessori's writings there
are frequent biblical references and
analogies. Her concept of "incarnation" is a
pertinent instance. Analogous to the
Christian mystery of Incarnation--that "the
Word was made flesh and dwelt among us"--is
the mystery found "in the birth of every
child, when a spirit enclosed in flesh comes
to live in the world."[41] Through this analogy

Montessori is suggesting that a spiritual, almost divine, aspect of the child takes its form in and through the physical aspects. Recalling the mental/physical categorization of potentialities, one can understand "incarnation" to be the mental or psychic potentialities as developed through the physical potentialities.

> We can now describe a child's psychic and physiological growth as a kind of "incarnation," understanding by this word that mysterious force which animates the helpless body of a newborn child, enables him to grow, teaches him to speak, and thus perfects him.[42]

> This fashioning of the human personality is a secret work of "incarnation." The child is an enigma. All that we know is that he has the highest potentialities, but we do not know what he will be. He must "become incarnate" with the help of his own will.[43]

The impetus for the "animation of the helpless body" mentioned here is a "mysterious," natural force, a notion central to Montessori's point of view because it suggests a "natural course" for the development of the personality and subsequently for the formation of character.

To bring into focus this natural course of development, the related concepts of "spiritual embryo" and "inner urges" must be clarified.

An embryo is an organism in its early stages of development. The physical embryo refers to the child in the embryonic period within the unique environment of the mother's womb. To parallel this notion of physical embryo, Montessori uses the term SPIRITUAL EMBRYO as an indication of the spiritual or psychic beginnings of the newborn child--a conceptualization of the child's burgeoning potentialities during the infancy period. In Childhood Education, Montessori describes the infant as an embryo "in whom the psychical powers and organs" are in an undeveloped stage:

> Could we not call the child, who
> in appearance only is psychically
> inert, an embryo, in whom the
> psychical powers and organs of
> man are being developed? He is
> an embryo in whom exists nothing
> nothing but nebulae that have the
> power to develop spontaneously
> certainly, but only at the expense
> of the environment--an environment
> rich in greatly different forms
> of civilization. That is why the
> human embryo must be born before

> completing itself and why
> it can reach further devel-
> opment only after birth. Its
> potentialities, in fact, must be
> stimulated by the environment.
>
> There will be many "inner
> influences" just as in physical
> growth there are many, especially
> during the processes depending on
> the genes, e.g., the influence
> of various hormones. In the
> spiritual embryo, instead, there
> are directing sensitivities.[44]

The latent potentialities must develop at "the expense of the environment," the environment being the necessary occasion for their growth. Moreover, the child possesses "sensitivities" which provide direction, so that just as genes guide the physical development during the first embryonic period, so also do "inner sensitivities" guide the psychic development of the spiritual embryo during the infancy period. Thus, the term SPIRITUAL EMBRYO indicates the child's mental and physical potentialities as burgeoning during the infancy period.

Involvement too in the discussion of the notions of incarnation and spiritual embryo is Montessori's reference to a "mysterious force" which has a decisive influence of the child's potentialities. Montessori recognizes a degree of order in the behavior of children. After comparing the order in children's behavior to that manifested in the celestial pattern, she concludes that, as the stars obey the "laws that govern the universe," so also man must obey the laws that govern the process of his development. Thus, Montessori states that the aim of education is to foster the "harmonious growth of all the potentialities of the child according to the laws of its being."[45] For since the natural laws of development are revealed through the child himself, it is the child's INNER URGES which guide his development and consequently reveal the natural path.

Montessori then sets out to determine the laws directing the child's formation, and discovers them by affording the child himself the opportunity to reveal them to her.

> Who, then, can reveal the natural ways along which the psychic development of man proceeds but the child himself, once he is placed in conditions permitting him to do so?
>
> Our first teacher, therefore, will be the child himself, or rather the vital urge with the cosmic laws

> that lead him unconsciously. Not
> what we call the child's will,
> but the mysterious will that
> directs his formation--this
> must be our guide.[46]

This "mysterious will" or "vital urge" is Nature, suggesting the path of development. Montessori describes this inner influence as "nebulae" and draws an analogy of their influence to that of one's genes in the initial cell:

> The nebulae are like mysterious
> potentialities comparable to those
> genes in the germinal cell that
> have power to direct the future
> tissues so that they can form
> complicated and structurally
> complete, determined organs.[47]

Nebulae, the concept of a guiding influence or impulse, suggest a greater degree of form and less mysteriousness than the concept of "vital urge." Montessori is alluding to an advance from a formless inner impulse to a more physical sensitivity, a progression further developed by her description of "vital urge" as a "sensitive period."

The so-called "vital urge" or guiding impulse is described by Montessori as a "special sensibility"; that is, a periodic disposition, and in the formulation of this notion she acknowledges the influence of the Dutch scientist Hugo de Vries.

> The Dutch scientist Hugo de Vries discovered these sensitive periods in animals, but it was we, in our schools, who discovered that they are also to be found in children and can also be used in teaching. A sensitive period refers to a special sensibility which a creature acquires in its infantile state, while it is still in a process of evolution. It is a transient disposition and limited to the acquisition of a particular trait. Once this trait, or characteristic, has been acquired, the special sensibility disappears. Every specific characteristic of a living creature is thus attained through the help of a passing impulse or potency. Growth is therefore not to be attributed to a vague inherited predetermination but to efforts that are carefully guided by periodic, or transient, instincts. These give direction by furnishing an impulse towards a determined kind of activity that can differ notably from that of the adult of the species.[48]

The concept "sensitive period" is an elaboration of the inner urge as a sensitivity or stage in one's development in which a characteristic is most likely to be acquired. Thus, nature's guiding hand takes the form of a "transient disposition" or "special sensibility."

Montessori employs the terms "mysterious will," "nebulae," and "sensitive period" in describing nature's directing influence in the process of the child's development. These three concepts not only describe a guiding impulse, but also suggest a movement from a "mysterious" inner realm toward the observable outside world. "Mysterious will" suggests an innermost, vital urge. "Nebulae" is the term which describes the vital impulse as "mysterious potentialities comparable to those genes in the germinal cell." This suggests a movement from the mysterious, formless urge toward a more concrete potentiality. While nebulae are the "mysterious" influences suggesting an "innermost" urge, they are also described as "potentialities" comparable to genes, suggesting an energy less mysterious than the "inner urge." The concept "sensitive period" involves an impulse which is both an inner phenomenon as well as a disposition relative to the external world. The vital impulse, as sensitivity, both initiates and guides the organism in its contact with the outer world. Of the three, the sensitive period concept has the most external disposition, and the concepts "mysterious will," "nebulae," and "sensitive period" are described by Montessori with a decreasing degree of "mysteriousness" and an increasing degree of form.

Since in her search for the laws governing the child's formation, Montessori discovered that the growth of one's potentialities proceeds according to natural staged or sensitive periods, she attributes the phenomenon of growth not to a "vague inherited predetermination, but to efforts that are carefully guided by periodic, or transient, instincts."[49] Natural development must be understood to involve both the efforts of the child and "periodic instincts," or a sequence of sensitive periods. Montessori's concept of these sensitive periods serves to give specific form to the notion of natural development, which she describes as a transient and staged development. Moreover, the stages themselves represent an <u>invariant</u> and natural aspect of growth, while the <u>variables</u> in growth are primarily the individual efforts of the child and his environmental circumstances. Montessori's notion of growth, and subsequently her method of education, emphasize the differences in degrees of development as related more to environmental circumstance and individual effort than to hereditary factors.

Montessori determined that the natural development of a child takes place (1) patterned according to stages of development, (2) guided by sensitive periods, and (3) occasioned by constant environmental circumstances. However, the actual cause of one's growth is the satisfaction of an inner urge. If one's urge is satisfied by suitable environmental conditions, then growth will occur. As will be seen in more detail later, the satisfaction of an urge causes growth, whereas the environmental stimuli are the occasion for this satisfaction.

Montessori's method of education, then, is an attempt to follow the path enlightened by our knowledge of the natural course of development. Accordingly, a single, uniform method of education is possible. This was Montessori's belief: that it is possible to conceive a "universal movement" for human reconstruction that follows a "single path."[50]

In Summary: Montessori's notion of character involves virtuous traits only. Although she occasionally uses the term character in a way that encompasses both deviant and virtuous behavioral traits, her most consistent and understandable reference is to virtuous behavior only. Behavior, whether virtuous or deviant, is the expression as well as the result of the organization of personality. Character, or virtuous behavior, results from a healthy organization of personality; whereas a lack of character, or deviant behavior, results from an unhealthy organization. Realizing this fact, one can understand that the formation of character corresponds to the organization of personality. How is personality organized? According to Montessori, personality development is occasioned by the environment. If one's personality interacts with suitable conditions, a healthy organization is fostered. If one's personality interacts with obstacles, an unhealthy organization results. Moreover, personality development is caused by the satisfaction of an inner impulse; hence her distinction between the environment, which is the occasion, and the satisfaction of the impulse, which is the cause. Furthermore, personality development is guided along a natural course by "inner urges." Scientific observation of these urges offers the possibility of a single, uniform, natural pattern of development, such a pattern as Montessori believes her method of education represents.

CHAPTER 3

THE CONCEPT OF EDUCATION AND ITS RELATION TO
PERSONALITY AND CHARACTER

Montessori addressed the education of
the individual at the International School of
philosophy in Amersfoort on December 28,
1937. The following extended quotation
displays her vision of the salvation of
mankind through the development of the human
personality.

> Education is indispensable not to
> foster material progress but to
> save humanity, and all our efforts
> must be directed toward helping
> the inner man form himself rather
> than fighting against the out-
> side world . . . . The aim of edu-
> cation should not be to teach how
> to use human energies to improve
> the environment, for we are
> finally beginning to realize that
> the cornerstone of education
> is the development of the human

personality and that in this
regard education is of immediate
importance for the salvation of
mankind. The environment must
promote not only the freedom of
the individual, but also the
formation of a society. The education of humanity must rest on
a scientific foundation and follow
from it every step of the way.
The levels of education must have
a foundation, a human aim--the
progressive development of the
child's personality, which our
experience with him has made us
see in an entirely new light; for
the child is free to act and to do
so without being influenced by the
suggestion exercised by the adult
shows us the real laws of life.[51]

The reconstruction of a humane society is
contingent upon the strength and unification
of the human personality, the full
elaboration of which depends upon a method of
education rooted in the laws of development.

Montessori spoke repeatedly of the need
totally to develop one's personality. In The
Child in the Church she defines the aim of
education as:

. . . a total development
of the personality, a harmonious growth of all the
potentialities of the child,
physical and mental, according
to the laws of it being.[52]

In Montessori's view, education is an aid to

the optimum and total development of an individual's physical and mental potentialities; and to assist in the physical sphere, she developed a unique sequence of manipulatable objects and activities. While insisting on the importance of sensory-motor development, her notion of totality did not exclude the intellectual, volitional, affective, and moral aspects of mental growth. Thus, she maintained that the totality of one's potentialities, mental and physical, lie within the scope of education.

In her insistence that education aims at the "harmonious" growth of one's potentiality, Montessori recognized the need to interrelate the physical and mental potentialities. She recognized also the need to interrelate the varied mental potentialities. The will, for example, must be appropriately influenced by intelligence and morality so as properly to guide one's activity. Similarly, one's feelings must be in harmony with intellectual and moral progress. According to Montessori, one's feelings, which are nature's means of influencing development, must be the foundation of that development"if we are not to lead the child towards illusion, falsity and darkness." To remain in step with the natural processes, an individual's growth must be guided by his affective response. The harmonious development and coordination of his potentialities are clearly an essential aspect of Montessori's aim of education.

In Montessori's view, education is a process based on natural laws of growth and the Dottoressa labored to disclose that the healthy organization of personality follows those laws. But how does one discover the laws of growth? Montessori believed that a natural pattern could be experimentally determined by observing the child's natural impulses in an atmosphere of liberty, where his sensibilities reveal natural growth stages. Accordingly, it is not only possible but also desirable to establish a pattern of education according to the laws of his natural development. This pattern of child development is a fundamental aspect of Montessori's aim of education: to aid the harmonious growth of all the potentialities of the child according to the laws of natural development.

What precisely does Montessori mean by natural development? Essential to the notion

is her belief that the cause of development
is the satisfaction of a primitive impulse;
and she distinguishes between the
satisfaction of an impulse, which is the
cause of development, and the environment,
which is the occasion for development. This
distinction was suggested by her study of
sensitive periods.

> They (the sensitive periods) show
> us that a child's psychic devel-
> opment does not take place by
> chance, that it does not originate
> in external stimuli but is guided
> by transient sensibilities, that
> is, by temporary instincts
> intimately connected with the
> acquisition of specific traits.
> Although this takes place
> within an external environment,
> the environment itself is more
> of an occasion than a cause; it
> simply provides the necessary
> means for spiritual growth,
> just as a material environ-
> ment provides food and air for
> the development of the body.[53]

The cause of the growth of one's
potentialities is not the "external
stimulus," but is related rather to one's
"transient sensibilities." Thus, the
environment is "more of an occasion than a
cause." In Spontaneous Activity in
Education Montessori pinpoints the cause of

the organization of personality.

> It is in the satisfaction of
> this primitive impulse, this
> internal hunger, that the
> child's personality begins
> to organize itself and reveal
> its characteristics; just as
> the newborn infant, in nourish-
> ing itself, organizes its body
> and its natural movements.[54]

Her position is quite clear. Unlike the behaviorists, she attributes the cause of growth more directly to internal activities than to external circumstance, since the satisfaction of an impulse is the cause of growth. Her point of view most certainly does not diminish the importance of the external environment. On the contrary, the environment is of paramount importance, for it provides the means to satisfy an impulse. The environment is, thus, the occasion either for health development or for unhealthy development of one's potentialities. The role of environment, as occasion, is emphasized in the following passage from Spontaneous Activity in Education:

> We must not therefore set
> ourselves the educational
> problem of seeking means
> whereby to organize the
> internal personality of
> the child and develop

his characteristics; the
sole problem is that of
offering the child the
necessary nourishment.[55]

Thus, while making the distinction between the satisfaction of an impulse (the cause) and the environment (the occasion), Montessori emphasizes the vital role which the latter plays in the development of an individual's potentialities.

"Man is a fusion of personality and education, and education includes the series of experiences he undergoes during his life."[56] Man's growth is occasioned by his environment, and more specifically by the "active experiences" within his environment. The unit of personality. . . has to be built up and formed by active experiences in the real world, to which it is led by the laws of nature."[57] Clearly, the harmonious interrelation of the elements of personality are thus organized by the engagement of the individual in active experience with a nourishing environment. Above all, it is nature that initiates and guides one's experiences by means of inner sensibilities or sensitive periods. As was discussed earlier, one's inner sensibility is the mechanism by which nature guides the organism into contact with the external environment and in this way initiates active experiences.

Montessori labored to achieve a scientific understanding and description of experiences conducive to optimum growth. The series of experiences should not be the result of random selection but should rather be determined in accordance with the laws of nature. Furthermore, it is the child who reveals, through his inner sensitivities, both the appropriate environmental experiences and their proper sequence. Consequently, the child must be allowed the opportunity to reveal as well as to satisfy his inner urges. The organization of personality is therefore dependent upon "active experiences in the real world" as well as an atmosphere in which the child is free to act in accordance with his inner urges. Two essential aspects of an environment prepared for the healthy organization of personality are, therefore, (a) an atmosphere of liberty and (b) concrete objects corresponding to the inner sensitivities of the individual.

Montessori identifies an atmosphere of liberty as a necessary condition for the spontaneous development of the human personality.

> In order that the phenomenon
> (organization of personality)
> should come to pass, it is
> necessary that the spontaneous
> development of the child should
> be accorded perfect liberty; that
> is to say, that its calm and
> peaceful expansion should not
> be disturbed by the intervention
> of an untimely and disturbing in-
> fluence; just as the body of the
> newborn infant should be left
> in peace to assimilate its nour-
> ishment and grow properly.[58]

Her concept of liberty is defined, therefore, in terms of an opportunity for the child to act in accordance with his inner urges. He is allowed and ensured the freedom to act in accordance with the natural laws of development. Thus, it is "working in freedom" that a child has the opportunity to satisfy, as well as to reveal, the "natural wants of the inner life," and it was by allowing liberty that Montessori was able to develop an ordered sequence of didactic materials based on the laws of nature.[59]

The second essential factor of a healthy environment is the inclusion of

external objects corresponding to the
"formative tendencies" of the child.

> It is essential, therefore, to
> offer objects which correspond to
> its formative tendencies, in order
> to obtain the result which
> education makes its goal: the
> development of the latent forces
> in man with the minimum of strain
> and all possible fullness.[60]

It was noted earlier that the child has a
tendency or sensitivity for interaction with
his environment. A particular sensitivity
must be met with a corresponding object in
order that the related latent potentialities
may develop to the fullest. If objects are
to be suitable nourishment for growth, they
must correspond to the inner urges of the
child. The objects of development must be
"experimentally determined with reference to
the psychical evolution of the child." So
the objects not only must correspond to the
child's sensitivities, but also must keep
step with the increasingly higher forms.

> The external material, then,
> should present itself to the
> psychical requirements of the
> child as a staircase which helps
> him to ascend step by step, and
> on the steps of this staircase
> there will of necessity be disposed
> the means of culture, and of the

higher formation. Therefore the
psychical exercises require new
material, and this, if it is to
fulfill its purpose, must con-
tain new and more complex forms
of objects capable of fixing
the attention, of making the
intelligence ripen in the con-
tinual exercise of its own
energies, and of producing those
phenomena of persistence in
application and of patience to
which will be added elasticity,
psychical equilibrium, and
the capacity for abstraction
and spontaneous creation.[61]

The pedagogic instruments are described by
Montessori as a "staircase" of materials
which represent the means for the child's
ascent to higher levels of formation, and
which correspond to the evolution of his
inner sensitivities.

The materials and activities begin with
the child's initial stages and are designed
to correspond to his development throughout
advanced levels. Thus, Montessori devised an
ordered sequence of didactic materials
corresponding to the natural order of growth.
Her set of didactic materials is perhaps the
most significant aspect of her method. Not
only are the materials themselves
significant, but more important perhaps is
the notion of an ordered sequence of

instructional materials for an individualized educational environment.

> To bring about such a progress we must offer the child a systematic, complex material, corresponding to his natural instincts. Thus, for instance, by means of our sensory apparatus we offer the child a series of objects capable of drawing his instinctive attention to colors, forms, and sounds, to tactile and baric qualities, etc., and the child, by means of the characteristically prolonged exercises with each object, begins to organize his psychical personality, but at the same time acquires a clear and orderly knowledge of things.[62]

Not only do the objects keep step with the higher levels of formation, but they are also the means for presenting the whole of culture. So, in addition to the organization of the psychic personality, a "clear and orderly knowledge of things" is acquired as a result of the individual's interaction with the sequence of didactic materials. With the acquired knowledge of things comes the acquisition of new interests. The "primitive impulse" is thereby transformed into a "discerning interest."

> When a child has added a cognition to the primitive impulse which

directs his attention to external
things, he has acquired other
relations with the world, other
forms of interest; these are no
longer merely those primitive
ones which are bound up with a
species of primordial instinct,
but have become a discerning
interest, based upon the conquests of the intelligence.[63]

The inner sensibility to which the external
objects must correspond acquire additional
forms of interest through the individual's
relation with the world. In this manner the
didactic materials with which the child
interacts transform "an impulse into a
conscious and voluntary quest" for an
increasingly varied range of knowledge.

Montessori's sequence of didactic
materials is an attempt to aid the child in
the total development of his potentialities
according to the natural stages of
development. The ordered sequence of
didactic materials represents (a) a broad
spectrum of activities, (b) a set of
activities well sequenced, and (c) a set of
manipulatable objects suitable for fostering
sensory-motor development.

The full range of Montessori materials
takes into account the variety of mental and

physical potentialities. There are materials designed to foster one's fine and gross motor development as well as to develop and sharpen all of one's senses. Included also are activities and materials designed to promote the growth of one's various mental potentialities. The Montessori materials and environment can be used in a manner so as to foster total development.

The materials are generally well integrated. The well integrated nature of these materials creates continuity in the passages from one developmental stage to another, as well as a coordinated development of one's potentialities. For instance, the "pink cubes" are designed to develop fine motor control while acting also as an "indirect preparation" for future academic learning. So, in terms of fine motor control, the pink cubes are the introductory materials in an integrated sequence designed to foster fine motor coordination. Moreover, the pink cubes are interrelated with materials designed to develop other potentialities as well. For example, they introduce the unit of ten, the concepts large and small, and the notion of a progression according to a standard unit. Thus, these mathematically related concepts are introduced in party by the sensorial material--the pink cubes.

Although the language and mathematics materials are perhaps the most obvious examples of sequentially arranged materials, less obvious sequential arrangements exist for one's physical, volitional, social, and moral development. Thus, the Montessori materials and activities complement the sequential nature of development and the progressive acquisition of culture.

The materials are primarily manipulatable objects designed for the development and enhancement of the senses and sensory-motor knowledge. Although Montessori developed her educational program to be employed on all levels, including the primary, secondary, and university levels, the major portion of her detailed work was on the early childhood level (that is, with children zero to six years old). Thus, the majority of her materials are designed to foster sensory-motor knowledge and to convey it via interrelated sense modalities. The "sandpaper letters" illustrate this multi-sensory approach. The child employs the sandpaper letter "s" to learn what an "s" is and what it does. The child can hear the sound it makes. He can feel or touch the sandpaper outline. As he sees and touches it, he gains a memory of the form or shape and is involved in a specific motor movement (stereognostic and kinesthetic senses). Thus, the materials and their use convey knowledge to the child through various interrelated sense modalities.

The Montessori materials are designed to promote learning in the following areas: sensorial, practical life, the three R's, geography, science, and spiritual or religious life. The sensorial materials are particularly designed to foster the development and coordination of the senses, to provide a sensory-motor base for later academic learning. Montessori developed practical life exercises with the intention of assisting the child in his attempt to become independent. These develop the child's ability to perform a multitude of tasks related to his everyday life. The content of the remaining areas is sufficiently indicated by their titles. The didactic materials reflect the various aspects of culture and are clearly a well-integrated sequence, reflecting both the individual's potentialities as well as the full-range of knowledge and culture.

The essence of Montessori's method of education is therefore the "bestowal of the nourishment suitable to psychical liberty of development in the most perfect manner possible."[64]

The Montessori method of education was founded on the conviction that it is possible to determine experimentally the elements of a nourishing environment. In Montessori's view, "the thing to be exactly determined is: what is necessary and sufficient as a response to the internal needs of a life in process of development, that is, of upward progression, of ascent?"[65] A criterion is necessary in order to "exactly determine" those objects which are appropriate for the development of one's personality. The objects, "cannot be 'taken at random'; they represent the result of an experimental study." They are manifestations of the child.[66] The criterion used by Montessori was the "instantaneous psychical reaction" evoked by the simulus.

Montessori recalls in Spontaneous Activity in Education how she first discovered the criterion for evaluating the suitability of a stimulus. While she was observing in her Casa dei Bambini, she happened to notice a child of three, "deeply absorbed in a set of solid insets," who exhibited unusual "fixity of interest in an object" and "repetitiveness" with regard to the activity related to it. Thus, "concentration of attention" and "repetition of the related activity" were the tow-fold criterion discovered by Montessori. A stimulus, then, is judged suitable for a child's development if, when presented to the child, it evokes a concentration of his attention and sustains a repeated activity. This dual response represents an "instantaneous psychical reaction," the criterion for evaluating the appropriateness of a stimulus.

> It (pedagogic instrument)
> is . . . a stimulus which is
> itself determined by the
> psychical reactions it is
> capable of producing and
> maintaining permanently . . . .
> The psychical reaction which
> constitutes the sole basis

of comparison in the determination of the tests, is a
polarization of the attention, and
the repetition of the actions
related to it. When a stimulus corresponds in this manner
. . . it serves, not to measure
but to maintain a lively
reaction; it is therefore a
stimulus to the "internal"
formation. Indeed, upon such activity, awakened and maintained,
the accompanying organism initiates its internal elaboration
in relation to the stimuli.[67]

This fact of correspondence between
nature and the stimuli of development is the
foundation of education. In Montessori's
view, the ordered sequence of didactic
materials corresponds to the natural pattern
of development. This connection is due to
the selection of objects based on a criterion
rooted in nature. In what sense is the
criterion grounded in nature? The criterion,
which is an "instantaneous psychical
response," is a natural response evidencing
the satisfaction of an in internal impulse.
It is a natural or automatic response
indicating the growth of personality. The
fact that this criterion has its basis in
nature is that which warrants Montessori's
statement that the sequence of didactic

material corresponds to the natural growth pattern. This criterion, which links the didactic materials to nature, enables Montessori to claim the disclosure of a single, uniform, natural pattern of development.

It was noted earlier that the development of personality is initiated and guided by inner sensitivities. In a corresponding sense, education is an attempt to assist an individual's growth by offering objects suitable for the satisfaction of these inner impulses. Growth, then, is occasioned by active experience with the external environment. Montessori's notion of active experience (that is, physical activity or movement) is essential to the development of personality, since, as she maintains, movement is both that which makes development possible and that which expresses the elements of personality. In the following passage she describes the vital role of movement in the development of personality.

> . . . Through movement, (the child) acts upon his external environment and thus carries out his own personal mission in the world. Movement is not only an expression of the ego but it is an

> indispensable factor in the
> development of consciousness,
> since it is the only real means
> which places the ego in a clearly
> defined relationship with external
> reality. Movement, or physical
> activity, is thus an essential
> factor in intellectual growth,
> which depends upon the impres-
> sions received from outside.
> Through movement we come in
> contact with external reality,
> and it is through these contacts
> that we eventually acquire
> even abstract ideas. Physical
> activity connects the spirit
> with the world, but the spirit
> has need of action in a twofold
> sense, to acquire concepts and
> to express itself exteriorly.[68]

Thus, movement is the mechanism for uniting one's inner sensitivities with pedagogical instruments; it is also the mechanism by which the whole personality is able to express itself exteriorly.

Just as movement is necessary to develop the physical potentialities, so also is it necessary to develop the mental potentialities. For example, movement supplies the sensory--motor knowledge required for the acquisition of abstract ideas.

> Mental development must
> be connected with movement

and be dependent on it.[69]

> But in our new conception the view
> is taken that movement has great
> importance in mental development
> itself, provided that the action
> which occurs is connected with
> the mental activity going on.[70]

As an example of the importance of movement
in the development of the mental
potentialities, Montessori shows the role of
movement in the development of speech.

> In the development of speech, for
> example, we see a growing power of
> understanding go side by side with
> an extended use of those muscles
> by which he forms sounds and words
> . . . Movement helps the develop-
> ment of mind, and this finds
> renewed expression in further
> movement and activity. It
> follows that we are dealing with
> a cycle, because the mind and
> movement are parts of the same
> entity. The senses also take
> part, and the child who has less
> opportunity for sensorial activity
> remains at a lower mental level.[71]

Similarly, volition finds expression in
movement:

> The whole external expression of
> the will is contained in movement:
> whatever action man performs,
> whether he walks, works, speaks or
> writes, opens his eyes to look, or
> closes them to shut out a scene,

he acts by "motion." An act of
the will may also be directed
to the restriction of movement:
to restrain the disorderly movements of anger; not to give way
to the impulse which urges us to
snatch a desirable object from the
hand of another, are voluntary
actions. Therefore the will is
not a simple impulse towards
movement, but the intelligent
direction of movement.[72]

Montessori's position is clear. Only through movement is the personality--mental as well as physical abilities--able to perfect and express its abilities.

In the previous chapter, CHARACTER was defined as the behavioral expression of the well-developed and coordinated personality: character is the type of behavior resulting from a harmonious organization of the elements of personality. It was further noted that didactic materials initiate movement, which in turn fosters the development of the personality, with character being its expression. The criterion used by Montessori to determine the suitability of a material was the dual phenomenon of concentration of attention and repetition of activity. She explains that associated with the dual psychic response are the beginnings of virtuous behavioral qualities.

> This phenomenon (psychical
> response) gradually became common
> among the children: it may
> therefore be recorded as a
> constant reaction occurring in
> connection with certain external
> conditions, which may be deter-
> mined. And each time that such
> a polarization of attention
> took place, the child began to be
> completely transformed, to become
> calmer, more intelligent, and
> more expansive, it (the child)
> showed extraordinary spiritual
> qualities, recalling the phen-
> omena of a higher consciousness,
> such as those of conversion.[73]

The expression of virtuous behavioral traits is produced by and occurs simultaneously with the psychic response. Thus, the child who is concentrating his energies is one who is becoming more "calm," more "intelligent," and more "expansive." He is exhibiting character. Character, then, is the result of the organized personality, which in turn is the result of the satisfaction of an impulse. The cause, in turn, of the formation of character is ultimately attributed to an inner activity. Unlike the behaviorists who attribute the growth of behavior to external circumstances, Montessori attributes growth to inner activity, which essentially is occasioned by the environment, for the latter has created the opportunity for internal or psychic activity.

But what are these psychic activities which develop and coordinate the elements of personality? Generally speaking, they are the intellectual, volitional, affective, and moral activities related to an object. Put another way, the didactic materials are, in Montessori's view, the gymnasium for psychic activity. Just as one's muscles must be exercised to allow for a variety of movements, so also psychic activities are put in motion to foster full psychic development.

> Just as movement, the gymnastics of children, is necessary, because, as is well known, muscles which are not exercised become incapable of performing the variety of movements of which the muscular system is capable, so an analogous system of gymnastics is necessary to maintain the activity of the psychical life.[74]

The INTELLECTUAL ACTIVITIES occasioned by the "determined object" are those of "comparing, judging, deciding upon an act, and correcting an error." These activities are involved, for example, "when the child, occupied with the solid insets, places and displaces the ten little cylinders in their respective places thirty or forty times consecutively."[75] So, as the child continues this "complex exercise of his physical activities," he "makes way for an internal development."[76]

> Hence the solid insets are
> not intended to give the child
> a knowledge of dimensions, nor
> are the plane insets designed to
> give him a conception of forms;
> the purpose of these, as of all
> the other objects is to make the
> child exercise his activities.[77]

While the purpose of the didactic materials is first and foremost to afford psychical activity, a "definite knowledge . . . is a necessary result; and, indeed, it is precisely the sensory knowledge of dimensions, forms and colors, etc., thus acquired, which makes the continuation of such internal exercises in fields progressively vaster and higher, a possible achievement.,"[78]

VOLITIONAL ACTIVITY is a second type of psychic activity prompted by the Montessori environment. Montessori explains that the

didactic materials and an atmosphere of
liberty present a situation in which the
child is afforded the opportunity to make
decisions.   One's   "intellectual
acquisitions" act as a foundation for these
decisions and at the same time make the child
independent of the suggestions of others.
With this independence he can then make his
own decision.

> Our little children are
> constructing their own wills when,
> by a process or self-education,
> they put in motion complex
> internal activities of com-
> parison and judgment, and
> in this wise make their
> intellectual acquisitions with
> order and clarity; this is
> a kind of "knowledge" capable
> of preparing children to form
> their own decisions, and one
> which makes them independent of
> the suggestions of others; they
> can then decide in every act of
> their daily life; they decide to
> take or not to take; they decide
> to accompany the rhythm of a
> song with movement; they decide
> to check every motor impulse
> when they desire silence.[79]

Volitional activity aids in the development
of personality and is related to intellectual
activity. Related to both intellectual and
volitional activity is the capacity for an

emotional response.

An EMOTIONAL RESPONSE constitutes a
third psychic activity involved in the
organization of personality. A positive
emotional response accompanies those
activities which are conducive to the healthy
development of the personality. It was noted
earlier that a specific affective response
accompanies the satisfaction of an internal
impulse. In the matter of exercise with
didactic materials this affective response is
called pleasure.

> But the child who chooses the
> objects, and perseveres in their
> use with the utmost intensity
>
> of attention, as shown in
> the muscular contractions which
> give mimetic expression to
> his face, evidently experience
> pleasure, and pleasure is an
> indication of healthy functional
> activity; it always accompanies
> exercises which are useful[80]
> to the organs of the body.

Thus, a positive response accompanies
"satisfying" intellectual and volitional
activity. Such a response functions then as
an indicator of those activities conducive to
the organization of the personality. It acts
not only as an indicator of appropriate
psychic activity, but also as the basis of a

sound education. As was noted in Chapter I, education must "include a basis of feeling, and be built up thereupon, if we are not to lead the child towards illusion, falsity and darkness."[81]

MORAL ACTIVITY is a fourth type of psychic behavior which aids in the development of personality. This process of distinguishing between good and evil was explained in Chapter I according to two stages: the first involving a "learned pattern of behavior," the second, concerned with a "voice of conscience."

The child develops this discernment during his first six years of life by absorbing the habits and customs of the community. Subsequently, moral activity influences the individual's intellectual and volitional behaviors, since it has the impact of clarifying one's perceptions of the world and guiding one's acts of volition. It is thus a fourth activity involved in the organization of personality and is related to the other intellectual, volitional, and affective functions.

Montessori's criterion for distinguishing between good and evil, if closely scrutinized, generates some troublesome questions, the seriousness of which warrants a brief digression. The criterion for distinguishing good from evil during the first stage is a learned pattern of behavior relative to the individual's environment. The criterion in the second stage involves a "voice of conscience." In contrast to the situational or relative nature of the first, the "voice of conscience . . . bound up with life itself and not (with) acquired social habits," is one involving a quality of absoluteness.

> Our moral conscience is, like out intelligence, capable of perfection, of elevation; this is one of the most fundamental of its differences from the instincts of animals. The sensibility of the conscience may be perfected, like the aesthetic sense, till it can recognize and at last enjoy "good," up to the very limits of the absolute and also until it becomes sensitive to the very slightest deviations towards evil. He who feels thus is "saved"; he who feels less must be more vigilant, and do his utmost to preserve and develop that mysterious and precious sensibility which guides us in distinguishing good from evil. It is one of the most important acts

of life to examine our own consciences methodically, having as our souce of illumination not only a knowledge of moral codes, but of love. It is only through love that this sensibility can be perfected. He whose sense has not been educated cannot judge himself.[82]

According to Montessori, the voice of consciences is an "internal sensation which warns us of perils, and causes us to recognize the circumstances favorable life."[83] Her explanation as to how the sensibility of conscience is to be perfected is not presented with her usual scientific preciseness. She explains only that one's conscience is to be examined methodically, using a knowledge of moral codes and "love." The sensibility which guides us in distinguishing good from evil is a feeling that is to be perfected by introspection. An individual is to examine his moral activities with regard to moral codes and thus, by constant examination, to perfect his moral sensibility. This, however, does not suggest a level of absoluteness. Montessori states that it is only through "love" that the sensibility can be perfected. She does not explain how "love" does in fact enhance this sensibility; moreover, the nature of her term "love" is so vague that it is rendered useless as a description of the perfecting process.

Montessori's claim that the voice of conscience is a criterion involving the quality of absoluteness suggests an interesting question for the moral philosopher. Does Montessori establish a connection between the educated sensibility and the knowledge of absolute good and evil? The question of whether her definition of "voice of conscience" warrants the attribution of the quality of absoluteness, although rather intriguing, is not within the scope of this study.

In summary: the essence of education, according to Montessori, is to provide stimuli appropriate for the optimum development of an individual's total personality. By providing the child with an atmosphere of liberty and after carefully observing him, Montessori was able to discover and develop such stimuli. Using the instantaneous psychical response (that is, concentration of attention and repetition of action) provoked by objects in the environment, the Dottoressa was able to determine experimentally not only the appropriate materials, but also their natural and proper sequence. The didactic materials represent, then, a natural sequence of stimuli which provide the opportunity for movement or physical activities. Movement, the mechanism for putting one's inner urges into contact with the appropriate didactic material, plays in turn a major role in the development and coordination of the elements of personality. Just as it provides the opportunity for physical growth, it also initiates the psychic activity necessary for the development and coordination of the elements of personality. Physical activity, is moreover, the behavioral expression of personality. Insofar as one develops a health personality, one becomes a man of character. Finally, the formation of character is the result of the healthy organization of personality and ultimately the aim of education.

CHAPTER 4

SUMMARY AND DISCUSSION

The intent of this study is to organize
and to clarify Montessori's concept of
personality. The previous chapters represent
such an effort. The purpose of this chapter
is, first, to offer a summary of the
conceptual scheme detailed earlier; and
second, to discuss William Heard Kilpatrick's
The Montessori System Examined (1914) and
David Norbert Campbell's "A Critical Analysis
of William Heard Kilpatrick's The Montessori
System Examined" (1970) in light of the
conceptual scheme developed in this study.

Summary of Previous Chapters:
The concept of personality and its
organization is the essence of the Montessori
method. Virtually all those who have written
about Montessori and her "method of
education" have chosen to focus on classroom
procedure rather than on the foundation for

that procedure. This study attempts to fill this serious gap by providing an explication of her pivotal concept of personality.

PERSONALITY has been defined, according to Montessori's writings, as the totality of one's potentialities. These potentialities were categorized in the present treatise according to PHYSICAL and MENTAL abilities. The physical potentialities are a SYSTEM OF RELATIONSHIPS involving the BRAIN, SENSE ORGANS, and MUSCLES. The potency of these abilities was defined by way of contrast with those of the "vegetative system." The potency of the physical abilities is due primarily to their relationship with the mental abilities, particularly the will. The vegetative system lacks this vital relationship with the will and and is for the most part "constant" and "fixed." The PHYSICAL potentialities were discussed as in need primarily of separate development and then of coordination with the MENTAL potentialities.

These latter potentialities of personality were defined as one's INTELLECTUAL, VOLITIONAL, AFFECTIVE, and

MORAL abilities. The intellectual potentialities were characterized by acts of distinguishing, classifying, cataloguing, and processing facts, and in addition, by the powers of imagination and abstraction. The second category of mental potentialities was described as one's volitional energy; that is, will power, or the mental activity that directs the physical elements. According to Montessori, nature exerts its influence on the child through his "primitive impulses." This influence diminishes as the child's own will develops and coordinates with other mental abilities; and the evolution from impulsive activity to intelligently and morally guided activity corresponds to the construction of his will. The third category was defined in terms of an emotional response underlying the development of an individual's personality. Feelings of joy and satisfaction accompany those experiences conducive to the healthy development of personality; whereas experiences that do not satisfy a person's primitive impulses evoke feelings of frustration and incompleteness. The final category of mental potentialities

involves one's moral abilities, which denote
mental activity involved with conscious
decisions of right and wrong. Montessori's
writings disclose a progression in the nature
of an individual's moral activity. Decisions
of right and wrong progress from a "learned
pattern of behavior" to decisions based on an
"inner conscience," which causes us to
recognize the circumstances favorable to
life. The inner conscience is "bound up with
life itself and not with acquired social
habits," involving therefore, an absoluteness
not present in the learned pattern of
behavior.

Four additional sets of terminology,
referring to the various potentialities of
personality, were found in Montessori's
writings: first, "psychic energy and
movement"' second, "sentiment and direction
of his ideation"; third, "internal
personality" and "inner personality"; and
fourth, "reflex personality." Psychic energy
and movement are two constituent factors of
personality. Psychic energy refers to the
mental potentialities as interacting with the
physical potentialities. The harmonious

interaction of the two categories of potentialities produces coordinated movement. Thus to view psychic energy and movement as two constituent factors of personality is generally compatible with the mental/physical categorization, although to do so may cause confusion if pressed in detail. Montessori's description of "the sentiments of the individual and the direction of his ideation" was found, in the present study, to correspond to the affective and intellectual aspects of personality. These two aspects when combined with constancy, or will, constitute the "inner personality." The terms "inner personality" and "internal personality" were used interchangeably and with reference to the mental potentialities. Montessori distinguished between a "receptive" personality and an "active" or "reflexive" personality. Reflex personality describes in general a basic assumption regarding the nature of personality. It signifies specifically one's ability for psychical reflex activity; namely, an instantaneous psychical response. This psychical reaction in turn is used by

Montessori as a criterion for determining suitable external stimuli.

Personality, according to Montessori, expresses itself in either virtuous or deviant behavior. In its most consistent use, the term CHARACTER was determined to refer specifically to virtuous behavior. Montessori established a connection between a certain organization of personality and a certain type of resultant behavior. She noted that the healthy organization of personality expressed itself in terms of CHARACTER, that is, in virtuous behavioral traits, and that the formation of character is therefore contingent upon and is the result of healthy organization of the elements of personality.

The concepts of INCARNATION, SPIRITUAL EMBRYO, and INNER URGES were analyzed in an effort to introduce and to clarify the notion of the natural development of personality. Montessori used the analogy of "incarnation" to describe the process of the mental potentialities taking form in and through the physical potentialities. "Spiritual embryo" was used to signify the child's burgeoning potentialities during the infancy period. Natural laws which are revealed through the child's "inner urges" guide the development and organization of personality. This concept of inner urges was found to progress from an "inner, mysterious urge" to a "sensitivity" involving an inner phenomenon and a related tendency toward an aspect of the external environment. The child, in other words, has natural impulses which in the beginning are internal but, as the child develops, acquire a more external posture.

The purpose of education follows directly from Montessori's notion of personality and its development. EDUCATION was defined as an aid to the development and coordination of all the potentialities of personality according to the natural laws of growth. Montessori's view of education hinges on her belief that growth is due to an inner activity. An important distinction was made between the satisfaction of one's inner impulse, which is the cause of the organization of personality, and the environmental circumstance, which is the occasion for the organization of personality.

Her belief that growth is due to inner activity clearly placed her in opposition to the behaviorist's view of external causes of growth. Montessori, however, emphasized also the vital role of the environment in providing opportunity for the satisfaction of one's primitive urge. Specifically, she identified an "atmosphere of liberty" and "external objects" as necessary environmental conditions for the spontaneous development of personality. Her notion of liberty was restricted to an individual's freedom to act in accordance with the natural laws of development. Thus, the child should be allowed and ensured freedom to act in accordance with his inner urges. Montessori viewed selected external material as a necessary complement to one's inner sensitivities. Nature's guiding hand, through the child's inner sensibilities, directs the individual into contact with the didactic materials. This interaction of the individual and the materials causes both physical and mental activity, which is essential to the development and harmonization of the personality. In addition to being essential to growth, this activity is simultaneously the expression of the personality. Didactic materials, which act as a "gymnasium" for one's sensibilities, are determined by the psychical manifestations of the child's inner urges. According to Montessori, the criterion for determining the suitability of the object is an "instantaneous psychical response," namely, concentration of attention and repetition of activity. Utilizing this two-fold criterion of concentration and repetition, Montessori developed an ordered sequence of didactic materials corresponding to the natural order of development. She described her "pedagogic instruments," or didactic materials, as a "staircase" of materials which represent the means for the child's ascent to higher levels of formation and which correspond to the evolution of his inner sensitivities. Montessori maintained that the infant's primitive urges evolve as his mental potentialities develop and acquire information. Thus, a "primitive impulse" is transformed into a "discerning interest," and correspondingly the objects must develop in complexity and variety. Montessori explained that the didactic materials are the occasion for intellectual and volitional activities which simultaneously enhance their own development while serving to coordinate all the elements of personality.

Related to intellectual and volitional activities is the capacity for an emotional response. This positive effective response accompanies "satisfying" intellectual and volitional behavior and therefore can be used as an indicator of those activities suitable to the development and organization of the personality. Moral activity is the fourth type occasioned by the Montessori environment. It is described as that aspect of man's personality involved with conscious decisions of right and wrong. Montessori's notion of morality was described according to two stages: first, decisions made according to a learned pattern of behavior; and second, decisions made according to a voice of conscience. In Montessori's view, the voice of conscience is an internal sensibility capable of perfection, a sensibility representing a criterion capable of yielding absolute distinctions of right and wrong.

Discussion

In 1914, at the height of America's interest and enthusiasm in Montessori and her methods, William Heard Kilpatrick, an assistant professor at Teachers College, Columbia University, wrote a criticism of the Montessori. Although Kilpatrick was not alone in his dispraise of Montessori's method, his analysis is perhaps the best known, and was considered by many to be a devasting blow to the Montessori system. Kilpatrick's critique remained unanswered until David Norbert Campbell, a doctoral student at the University of Illinois at Urbana-Champaign, wrote a dissertation in 1970, entitled "A Critical Analysis of William Heard Kilpatrick's The Montessori System Examined." This section will first summarize Kilpatrick's criticism and then submit a synopsis and discussion of Campbell's analysis of that examination.

In his examination of the Montessori system Kilpatrick discusses seven issues:

    A.   Education as development

    B.   The doctrine of liberty

C. Adequacy of self-expression in The Montessori System

D. Auto-education

E. Exercises of practical life

F. Sense-training by means of the didactic apparatus

G. The School Arts: Reading, Writing, and Arithmetic

A. EDUCATION AS DEVELOPMENT

The purpose of Montessori's system of education, according to Kilpatrick, is the development of the individual. Kilpatrick views this development as involving two elements: "mastering the environment and expressing one's self." He faults Montessori's view of development as being incomplete; that is, being concerned only with the unfolding of the inner self.

> Education is thus, in truth,
> the completest possible
> development of the individual;
> but the task of securing such
> a development is as great as
> is the complex of civilization.
> Expression involves as truly
> the mastering of this complex
> as it does the living out
> of the impulsive life. More
> exactly, the two elements
> of mastering the environment
> and expressing one's self

are but outer and inner aspects
of one and the same process; each
either meaningless or impossible
apart from the other. Only in
this larger sense can it be said
that education is the development
of the individual. Some, on the
contrary, have taken the position,
previously suggested, that
in the child's nature as given
at birth there is contained--in
some unique sense--all that the
child is to become . . . . Such
is Madam Montessori's view.[84]

Kilpatrick interprets Montessori's view to be
a mere "unfolding" of that which is latent
within the individual. Kilpatrick warns of
the "danger" in such a view and suggests that
"such   a   theory   leads   easily,   if   not
inevitably, to Rousseau's opposition to man's
whole   institutional   life."[85]   Kilpatrick
concludes:

We must, therefore, reject Madam
Montessori's interpretation of
the doctrine of development as
inadequate and misleading. The
useful elements of this doctrine
are covered up in error whenever
development is identified with
the mere unfolding of latency.[86]

B.   THE DOCTRINE OF LIBERTY

The second issue discussed by Kilpatrick
is that of liberty; that is, "the degree to

which the child shall by his own choice determine his own activities at school.[87] Kilpatrick expressed his belief that a "relatively free expression of the child's natural impulses" is an "efficient plan for his proper rearing." Thus, he generally favors Montessori's insistence on an atmosphere of freedom. While in general agreement with her notion of freedom, he believes that her "prepared environment" does not provide situations for "adequate social cooperation." Thus, Montessori's "re-emphasis of the doctrine of freedom" is commendable, while her lack of appropriate environment for social development is reprehensible.

C. ADEQUACY OF SELF-EXPRESSION IN THE
   MONTESSORI SYSTEM

Kilpatrick criticizes Montessori's didactic materials as not providing adequate opportunity for self-expression:

> The didactic apparatus which forms
> the principal means of activity
> in the Montessori school affords
> singularly little variety . . . .
> But after all is said, the
> Montessori school apparatus affords
> but meager diet for normally
> active children . . . . Those more

advanced forms of self-expression, drawing and modeling, are,
on the while, inferior to what we
have in this country. Modeling
is, in fact, hardly at all in
evidence. Drawing and painting
are occasionally good, but
frequently amount to nothing but
the coloring of conventionalized
drawings furnished by the
teacher. Stories have little or
no place--a most serious oversight
. . . . On the whole, the imagination, whether of constructive
play or of the more aesthetic
sort, is but little utilized.[88]

Kilpatrick concludes that the Montessori curriculum does not allow for the expression of a large portion of the child's nature. The didactic materials, according to Kilpatrick, are "inadequate and unduly restrictive."

D. AUTO-EDUCATION

Kilpatrick recognizes that auto-education--that is, self-education--is a necessary correlative of a regime of freedom. He regards Montessori's strong belief in auto-education as appropriate and laudable. However, the specific materials, in Kilpatrick's opinion, do not adequately complement the notion of auto-education. In his view, the materials evoke a mechanical manipulative activity.

> The didactic apparatus is in
> intention so devised that with
> each piece one, and only one,
> line of activity is feasible . . .
> . It is
>   in this limited fashion
> that Madam Montessori provides
> self-education. It is under such
> conditions that the directress
> keeps herself in the background
> and relies upon the cylinder
> box to set the problem and test
> the solution. Surely it is a
> naive trust in a very generous
> transfer of training which
> can see appreciable profit
> in so formal and restricted
> a scheme of to-education.[89]

In place of these limited and restrictive materials, Kilpatrick would allow for real-life situations to present the occasion for self-education. For Kilpatrick it is in life itself and the situations that arise therefrom that we find abundant instances of evident self-education.[90] Although Kilpatrick agrees that auto-education is a valuable notion, he views Montessori's implementation as too "formal and restrictive."

E. EXERCISE OF PRACTICAL LIFE

Kilpatrick values Montessori's "practical-life exercises" insofar as they represent occupations of immediate utility. Once again Kilpatrick emphasizes the need for the school to function "more definitely as a social institution, adapting itself to its own environment and utilizing more fully actual life situations." Accordingly, Montessori's practical-life exercises are valuable insofar as they represent "real-life situations." Kilpatrick comments that these exercises must surely be modified according to the needs of the community.

F. SENSE-TRAINING BY MEANS OF THE DIDACTIC
    MATERIALS

Kilpatrick evaluates Montessori's "system of sense-training" by analyzing its theoretical base. He first identifies three general theories relative to sense-training and then associates Montessori's position with the first two. The three positions can be identified as follows:

1) that the sense organ itself can
    be improved by sense-training,

2) that the sense-organ itself is not
    changed, but rather, a new brain
    connection has been set up, and

3) that while a new brain connection
has been established, the new
power or faculty is not transferable to other areas of activity.
Thus, the training is specific
and not generally transferable.[92]

According to Kilpatrick Montessori apparently
"vacillates between the first and second
theories." Accordingly, she tends to agree
with the concept of the general transfer of
training and in the ability of the refinement
of senses. To Kilpatrick, Montessori's
agreement with the first two statements
indicates her belief in the "outworn and
castoff" faculty psychology theory.
Kilpatrick argues that there is "substantial
agreement" as to the validity of the third
statement, which substantially replaces the
outdated faculty psychology theory. He
concludes:

> . . . that Madam Montessori's
> doctrine of sense-training is
> based on an outworn and castoff
> psychological theory; that the
> didactic apparatus devised to carry
> this theory into effect is in so
> far worthless; that what little
> value remains to the apparatus
> could be better got from
> the sense-experiences incidental
> to properly directed play with
> wisely chosen, but less expensive
> and more childlike, playthings.[93]

G. THE SCHOOL ARTS: READING, WRITING, AND ARITHMETIC

In Kilpatrick's view, Montessori employed a phonetic approach to the teaching of reading, Its value to the American educational enterprise is negligible, according to Kilpatrick, as it "has nothing of novelty in it for America." What it can offer to America "has long been present with us, and a vogue previously won has for a decade been passing away."[94]

Kilpatrick redirects his focus to Montessori's belief in indirect preparation for writing. He comments specifically on two essential elements in the process of writing:

1) development of the muscular mechanism in writing, and

2) sensory knowledge of the visual-muscular image of the alphabetical signs.[95]

The Montessori materials designed to foster (1) and (2) may be a contribution, according to Kilpatrick, but final judment must be suspended until the results of further "discussion and experimentation" are available.

Kilpatrick's discussion, evaluation, and

criticism of Montessori's method of teaching
arithmetic is presented here in its entirety:

> As to arithmetic, there is little
> to be said. About the only novel-
> ty is the use of the so-called
> long stair. This consists of
> ten blocks, of lengths varying from
> one to ten decimeters, being in
> other dimensions the same. These
> are divided into decimeters,
> alternate divisions being painted
> in like colors. These blocks are
> used in teaching the various com-
> binations which sum ten. On the
> whole, the arithmetic work seemed
> good, but not remarkable; probably
> not equal to the better work done
> in this country. In particular
> there is very slight effort
> to connect arithmetic with
> the immediate life of the child.
> Certainly, in the teaching of
> the subject, there is for us
> no fundamental suggestion.[96]

Once again Kilpatrick finds "nothing novel"
in Montessori's work and furthermore suggests
that, as a rule, these subjects had better
not be taught prior to the age of six.[97]

Kilpatrick concludes his review of the
Montessori system by reiterating the various
tenets of her theory that are likewise held
by the Rousseau-Pestalozzi-Froebel group. He
then engages in a comparison of Montessori's
work with that of John Dewey in order to

"estimate" her worth from a different perspective. The comparison demonstrates, according to Kilpatrick, that "they are ill advised who put Madam Montessori among the significant contributors to educational theory. Stimulating she is; a contributor to educational theory, hardly, if at all."[98] Kilpatrick considers Montessori's most valuable service to be the founding of the Casa dei Bambini and her emphasis on the "scientific conception of education, and on the practical utilization of liberty."[99]

David Norbert Campbell's dissertation entitled "A Critical Analysis of William Heard Kilpatrick's The Montessori System Examined" (1970) is the first scholarly study of Kilpatrick's criticism. He introduces his analysis by providing background information on both Kilpatrick and the Montessori movement, and his second chapter presents a thorough and objective exposition of the seven points of Kilpatrick's critique. Campbell points out that Kilpatrick's most critical censure regards Montessori's "ignorance of the newer developments and thinking in psychology." Moreover, Campbell suggests that Montessori's notion of sense-training draws Kilpatrick's "greatest interest and his most damning criticism." In a rather concise and accurate manner he summarizes Kilpatrick's disapproval as follows:

> Kilpatrick's summation leaves
> little left to salvage of the
> Montessori System. She has proved
> stimulating by her advocacy of the
> scientific concept of education.
> her doctrine of unfolding
> is neither novel nor correct.
> In her doctrine of liberty there
> is no theoretical contribution,
> although our kindergarten
> and primary schools should take
> account of her achievements
> in this respect. Auto-education
> is a good term but an old idea.
> There is some value in "practi-
> cal life" activities. Perhaps
> the Casa dei Bambini is her
> greatest contribution. The sense-
> training is unacceptable except
> in a very modified degree and
> the didactic apparatus is also
> rejected. Her preparation for
> reading and writing should prove
> helpful in Italy; perhaps
> the writing method will be of
> some value everywhere. "Her
> greatest service lies probably
> in the emphasis on the
> scientific conception of
> education and in the practi-[100]
> cal utilization liberty".

The first issue taken up for discussion by Campbell is that of Montessori's psychology. Kilpatrick's most fundamental criticism is that Montessori adhered to and based her pedagogy on the out-dated "faculty psychology theory." Responding to the charge that Montessori was ignorant of contemporary psychological thought, Campbell points out that it was not a matter of being "unaware," but rather a matter of a different perspective--namely, physiological rather than psychological.

> It is not so much that Montessori
> was unaware of contemporary
> movements and theory in psychology,
> for she seems to have had at least
> a passing knowledge, as demon-
> strated here; but it is more
> likely that in her approach she
> displayed her totally different
> origin. Boyd describes her as a
> "sensationalist," i.e., in the
> medical tradition of approaching
> mind through body, that, she
> thinks of mind as beginning
> in purely physiological pro-
> cesses, developing into sensory-
> motor activities, and finally,
> "attaining the higher forms
> of mentality, each successive
> stage differing from its pre-
> decessor in character." It is
> vital to note once again that
> Montessori's training was in

medicine. There is a distinct
possibility that Boyd is quite
correct, i.e., that Montessori
never really thought in our usual
psychological terms at all.[101]

In addition to the influence of her medical
training, Campbell notes the psychological
orientation of Itard and Seguin, both of whom
had a significant influence on Montessori's
method. As to the charge that Montessori
tended to adhere to faculty psychology,
Campbell responds:

Nowhere in actual practice, in
the directions given for the
use of the didactic materials,
in the historical foundation
of her doctrine, no matter
how weak philosophically or
psychologically, is there any
real evidence that Montessori
believed in or advocated faculty
psychology in the sense Kilpatrick
charged or according to the Smith,
Stanley, Shores description.[102]

Campbell defined faculty psychology according
to the following four propositions delineated
by Smith, Stanley, and Shores:

1) . . . that man is endowed at birth
    with something called mind or soul
2) . . . that this mind or soul
    operates through distinct
    faculties or powers

3)   . . . that these powers can be
     improved and developed by exercise

4)   . . . that subjects such as
     Latin or mathematics are
     especially well suited for
     such exercises and that each
     faculty can, when properly
     disciplined, be equally useful on
     any appropriate material. [103]

Campbell points out that these propositions are not congruent with Montessori's beliefs nor her practices and also that, for Kilpatrick's charge to be valid, it must be proved that she believed that her sense-training was transferable.[104] Campbell notes that "no such claim is ever made by Montessori," and that sense-training in Montessori's view is only a 'preparation' for intellectual training.[105] Campbell cites a 1948 statement of Montessori that articulates clearly her belief that the mind is a unified whole and "virtually connected with the whole personality."

The second aspect of Kilpatrick's stricture of Montessori's psychology taken up by Campbell relates to "unfolding" for the child. Campbell responds that Montessori never used the term unfolding. Furthermore, through a careful explication of related terminology—such as inner directives and sensitive periods—he attempts to establish that there is nothing in the notion of developmental periods which would support a belief in predetermined development or unfolding in the sense used by Kilpatrick.[106] Engaging Montessori's obscure discussion of this topic, Campbell labors to demonstrate that the mysterious process of unfolding is one in which the child's "hidden" abilities become manifest if given the "proper environment." Thus, the manifestation of one's hidden abilities is due to "multifold causes." While they seem to emerge "mysteriously," it does not follow that their development is predetermined. Campbell ultimately discounts Kilpatrick's presumption of Montessori's adherence to the "faculty psychology" theory and to her belief in the process of "unfolding" according to a predetermined pattern.

> She did not then, practice faculty
> psychology, as we commonly
> understand that theory. Nor
> did she believe in "unfolding" in
> the child according to some pre-
> determined pattern, although
> perhaps, partially due to her con-

tinuing and deeply felt religious
beliefs, she did view the young
child as possessing amazing
abilities to do intellectual
work which seemed mysterious[107]
--at least to Montessori.

Next, Campbell analyzes the general
aspects of Kilpatrick's critique with
reference to the "prevailing doctrines of
American education in 1914, and the decline
of the Montessori Movement."[108] Campbell
evaluates Kilpatrick's charges:

1) that there was little or no
    allowance made in the Montessori
    system for games, aesthetic[109]
    creation and imagination.

2) that the Montessori environment
    did not provide for "adequate
    social cooperation," and

3) that perhaps the teaching of
    reading and writing is not useful
    or desirable at such an early age.

Regarding Montessori's position on play
and creative experiences, Campbell recalls
that she did not consider her students
"babies" with "inferior personality" and
therefore did not approach them with "games"
and "foolish stories." Campbell
characterizes the nature of Montessori's
system as "marked by a seriousness, by a work
ethic, by an impatience with aimless activity

and play for the sake of play.[110] Montessori discovered that the child regarded work as pleasurable and therefore preferred "what we commonly call work." Thus, Campbell states "work is play for Montessori and she finds no good reason to create fantasies for children."[111] While Montessori's emphasis is on a "scientific" or "factual" view of reality, she did provide opportuntiies for "games, songs, and work with clay, modeling and design." Certainly Montessori's belief in the necessity for a solid grounding in reality and her belief that children prefer "work" over "aimless play" led to a de-emphasis on games, songs, and aimless play.

Campbell responds to Kilpatrick's criticism of Montessori's lack of opportunities for social cooperation by noting that Montessori was indeed aware of the "need for social interaction." Moreover, she "believed that her method 'prepared' the child for socialization."[112] Admittedly her method is more "individual-oriented" than the "group-oriented" kindergarten. First of all Montessori's notion of socialization is

different from Kilpatrick's and, second, her
environment provides less organized group
activity than the kindergarten.

Campbell counters Kilpatrick's queries
regarding the desirability of teaching
reading and writing skills at such an early
age with the following remarks:

> The "explosion" or seemingly
> sudden ability to write is hardly
> surprising when one considers
> the preparation for it, for there
> is a long, unhurried process with
> letter-tracing and other very
> definite preparatory exercises.
> However, Montessori saw
> the reading reading and writing
> skills as only one outcome of
> her method and not to be over-
> emphasized or taken out of the
> total Montessori experience.[113]

Campbell fortifies his position in a later
chapter when he discusses the current
research in preschool education which
suggests the importance of such experiences
in the early years.

Campbell concludes his analysis of
Kilpatrick's investigation with the view
that, considering his "severity," his
criticism was "not that total." Kilpatrick
did not "bring himself to totally discredit"
the positive aspects of liberty and

scientific investigation. Kilpatrick's faultfinding, according to Campbell, focused on Montessori's belief in "wrong theory."[114] Finally, Campbell states that possibly the only charge that is substantial was that of "rigidity."[115]

> It is the rigidity of the use of the didactic materials, the restrictions regarding games, play and imagination, the reliance on and adherence to the original ideas of Montessori which allowed no variance and expansion which could not withstand the open-endedness of Dewey's philosophy.[116]

Having assessed Kilpatrick's review, Campbell focuses on the validity of the aforementioned aspects of the Montessori system as judged in light of contemporary research in child psychology and child development. Generally speaking, recent findings substantially support many of Montessori's ideas and practices. From his perusal of the research Campbell concludes:

> Undoubtedly the Montessori Method incorporates a great deal of what many experts and educators are presently assuming should be part of an effective preschool educational system. What research has been accomplished seems to

indicate substantial amount of
support for many of Montessori's
ideas and practices.[117]

Campbell's own words can perhaps best
conclude his evaluation of Kilpatrick's
reproof.

> In regard to Kilpatrick's criti-
> cism, which has formed the basis
> for this study, it should be
> evident that in general it was
> somewhat exaggerated, a bit
> premature and not terribly
> objective. As already noted,
> Kilpatrick was certainly justified
> in several of his criticisms,
> especially those regarding
> aesthetic experiences and games.
> In other aspects one cannot escape
> the feeling he was searching too
> hard for faults and should have
> instead understood, with some
> deeper perspective, that there was
> not that much to understand and
> criticize, and that he was dealing
> with a method which, like most
> practically derived educational
> methods, may have been weak in
> theory but at least workable and
> able to demonstrate a degree of
> success, or it would have never
> been heard of in the first place.
> At least in the case of Montessori,
> there was not much scientific
> openness and objectivity displayed
> by Kilpatrick. The scientific
> attitude which everyone was
> proclaiming was not evident in

> practice, for if it had been,
> Montessori might have been given an
> opportunity to prove her method.[118]

Is Campbell accurate in his analysis of Kilpatrick's criticisms? According to the delineation of Montessori's theory and practice detailed in the previous chapters, Campbell's analysis is substantially correct. While his analysis is generally accurate, he overlooked the fundamental unity of Montessori's position; namely, her psychological foundation. Campbell did not sift through the Biblical metaphors, the mystical-type prose, the rambling narration, and the often piece-meal description of her theoretical position. Generally speaking, William H. Kilpatrick's failure to examine thoroughly Montessori's writings manifests itself in the common view, also held by Campbell, that the Montessori Method is "just that--a method." Campbell erroneously concludes that her method is "derived from successful operation and not from a well thought out, systematic philosophy or psychology."[119] Or again, Campbell points out Kilpatrick's probable frustration at "discovering that there was indeed no systematic philosophy or psychology forming a base for the Montessori Method."[120] Quite the contrary is true. Although her presentation was often piecemeal, she did have a definite psychological foundation. The delineation of Montessori's concept of personality and its relation to character and education is evidence that Montessori did indeed have in mind a "definite" psychology, although it may not always have been internally consistent or even correct. Furthermore, her psychology served as the foundation for her method. Perhaps the piecemeal presentation of her ideas and practices contributed to the difficulty of recognizing her psychological scheme, but certainly a systematic psychology existed. As campbell aptly pointed out, however, her orientation was physiological, not psychological.

Campbell began his analysis by addressing Kilpatrick's most fundamental criticism; namely, Montessori's adherence to the out-dated faculty psychology. Campbell corrected Kilpatrick by stating that Montessori did not practice nor did she believe in faculty psychology. Campbell identified the real issue as being whether or not Montessori believed that sense-training was transferable, and his conclusion that sense-training is only a preparation for intellectual development is consistent with our previous discussion regarding mental and physical potentialities. These potentialities must be developed and, as parts of a unified whole, must then be harmonized. Only through physical activity is one able to satisfy the inner impulses, the satisfaction of which causes the development and harmonization of the potentialities; and providing the opportunity for this satisfaction is the primary purpose of the didactic materials. Moreover, the acquisition of skills and cognitions is of secondary importance, and functions as an indirect preparation for further development.

Montessori was also censured by Kilpatrick because of her alleged belief in the predetermined "unfolding" of that which is within. In this regard Campbell substantiates two points. First, Montessori never used the term unfolding; and secondly, there is nothing in her notion of developmental stages which supports a belief in a predetermined development.

some additional comments should be made regarding Kilpatrick's criticism. First regarding his afore-mentioned link of Montessori with the faculty psychology view; the Dottoressa maintained that growth is due to the individual's interacting with his environment while simultaneously following definite stages. Her psychology is more characteristic of the developmental-interactionist point of view than the faculty psychology view. Secondly, Kilpatrick repeatedly aligns Montessori with the Rousseauian tradition relative to the notion of unfolding an individual's latent potentiality. The danger, according to Kilpatrick, was that adherence to such a theory would lead "easily, if not inevitably, to Rousseau's opposition to man's whole institutional life." But Montessori does not fit into the Rousseauian tradition in this regard. Neither is this her view of development, nor does she oppose man's whole institutional life. Both the individual's potentialities and his environment influence his growth. The child does not escape from civilization, but rather engages it. He is offered, not the absence of culture so as to unfold according to nature, but is provided all the advantages of the Casa dei Bambini. In fact, her sequence of didactic materials was designed to present the totality of one's culture. Her prepared environment includes a "staircase" of materials by which the child is led to the heights of personal and cultural development, a reality that is proof positive of her acceptance of institutional life.

Campbell's counter-point to Kilpatrick's view that there are too few opportunities for "games, aesthetic creation, and imagination" was an explanation of Montessori's serious, work-oriented approach to education. Campbell describes Montessori's view regarding work and play, and emphasizes her belief in the child's preference for work. Although he explains Montessori's rationale for the de-emphasis of games and fantasy, Campbell tends to accept the validity of

Kilpatrick's criticism.

Montessori's own response to Kilpatrick's charge might have been much stronger insofar as her belief in the child's preference for work was based on the "natural laws of growth" as revealed by the child. According to Montessori, the didactic materials were experimentally determined. They were chosen because of their capacity to satisfy one's inner impulses. Thus, it was the response of the children that led Montessori to the conclusion that the child preferred work over aimless play and that this preference was initially a "natural" preference and subsequently a preference due to a "discerning interest."

Campbell's distinction between Montessori's notion of socialization and that of Kilpatrick was quite appropriate. Montessori was not only aware of the need for socialization, as Campbell points out, but she made it an integral part of her system. Her position is individual-oriented and based upon freely chosen social engagement rather than required, organized group activity. In addition to this fundamentally divergent point of view, Montessori considered the sensitive period for socialization to occur much later. Montessori explained the education of the individual according to four levels in her book Education and Peace. She conceived of social formation as following the development of one's individuality, for only when the child has cultivated his individuality, is he capable of experiencing "every aspect of social life."

Campbell aptly reviews the current thinking in early childhood education, which overwhelmingly supports the teaching of reading and writing skills during the early years. He reminds the reader, moreover, that the reading and writing skills are "only one outcome of her method and not to be overemphasized or taken out of the total Montessori experience."[121]

Summarizing his analysis of Kilpatrick's charges, Campbell characterizes them as "somewhat exaggerated, a bit premature, and not terribly objective." In the view of the present writer, Campbell sufficiently documents his conclusions. In the light of the psychological scheme provided by our study, it should be emphasized that Kilpatrick had misinterpreted and was generally mistaken in his understanding of Montessori's views, especially with regard to her theories of development and sense-training.

In summary:

In his analysis of Kilpatrick's criticism, Campbell focused initially on the central issues, presented an objective and thorough exposition, and finally offered a well-documented rebuttal. His criteria for evaluation were primarily historical analysis, and contemporary research in early childhood education. Montessori's psychological scheme organized in the context of the present study corroborates Campbell's demonstration of Kilpatrick's misinterpretation and invalid conclusions.

A final but essential point must be made at this time. Campbell himself was misled by Montessori's unsystematic and oftentimes inconsistent presentation of her views. The following statement in Campbell's conclusion suggests his misconception of the thrust of Montessori's work.

> (The) Montessori Method is just
> that--a method. And like many
> successful methods it was derived
> from successful operation and not
> from a well thought out, systematic
> philosophy or psychology.[122]

Given the previous explication of
Montessori's psychology, the above statement
suggests an incomplete understanding of
Montessori's theoretical position. The
Dottoressa clearly states that to understand
the Montessori method, the name "method"
should be eliminated. She emphasizes that
one "must consider the human personality and
not a method of education."[123] The issue
with Campbell's characterization of the
Montessori method as "just a method" is not a
semantic one. The argument is not a
superficial one, but concerns the essence of
Montessori's position. Her constant and
guiding concern was the "human personality."
Her efforts were an attempt to understand its
nature and its manner of development. Her
system of education was simply a "help given
in order that the human personality may
achieve its independence."[124] Her system of
education was a response to her understanding
of the nature and development of human

personality. Her "method of education" was most certainly developed from and consistent with her notion of man and his pattern of growth. Her own assertion stressed, in fact, that her method was "more than a general method of instruction."

> More fundamental than this, its object is to influence the whole life of the child: it aims, in short, at a total development of the personality, a harmonious growth of all the potentialities of the child, physical and mental, according to the laws of its being.[129]

Thus, to understand the Montessori method is to understand Maria Montessori's concept of personality.

FOOTNOTES

INTRODUCTION

1. Maria Montessori, "A Centenary Anthology 1870-1970" (Amsterdam: Association Montessori Internationale, 1970), p.9.

2. Maria Montessori, The Montessori Method, with an Introduction by Hunt (New York: Schocken Books, 1964), p. 33.

3. Ibid., p. 33.

4. Maria Montessori, Childhood Education (Chicago; Henry Regnery Company, 1974), p. 8.

CHAPTER I MONTESSORI'S CONCEPT OF PERSONALITY

5. Maria Montessori, The Child in The Church (London: Sand & Company, 1930), p. 141.

6. Maria Montessori, Absorbent Mind (New York: Holt, Rinehart, & Winston, Inc., 1949), p. 136.

7. Ibid., p. 140.

8. Maria Montessori, The Secret of Childhood (Notre Dame, Indiana: Fides Publishers, Inc., 1936), p. 43.

9. Montessori, The Child in the Church, p. 141

10. Maria Montessori, Education and Peace (Chicago: Henry Regnery Co., 1972), p. 131.

11. Montessori, Absorbent Mind, p. 94

12. Montessori, Absorbent Mind, p. 137.

13. Montessori, The Secret of Childhood, p. 119.

14. Montessori, Absorbent Mind, pp. 86-8.

15. Maria Montessori, Spontaneous Activity in Education (New York: Schocken Books, 1965), p. 198.

16. Ibid., p. 205.

17. Montessori, Absorbent Mind, p. 184.

18. Ibid., p. 253.

19. Ibid., p. 142.

20. Montessori, Spontaneous Activity in Education, p. 171.

21. Ibid., pp. 184-5.

22. Ibid., p. 331.

23. Montessori, Absorbent Mind, p. 129.

24. Ibid., p. 194.

25. Ibid., p. 189

26. Ibid.

27. Montessori, Spontaneous Activity in Education, p. 337.

28. Montessori, The Secret of Childhood, p. 189.

29. Montessori, Spontaneous Activity in Education, P. 178.

30. Ibid., pp. 195-6.

31. Ibid., pp. 72-3.

CHAPTER II CHARACTER AS THE HEALTHY ORGANIZATION OF PERSONALITY

32. Montessori, Absorbent Mind, p. 129.

33. Montessori, Childhood Education, p. 94.

34. Montessori, Absorbent Mind, pp. 218-9.

35. Montessori, The Secret of Childhood, p. 201.

36. Montessori, Absorbent Mind, p. 196.

37. Ibid., p. 213.

38. Montessori, Spontaneous Activity in Education, p. 178.

39. Ibid.
40. Montessori, Absorbent Mind, p. 193.

41. Montessori, The Secret of Childhood, p. 35.

42. Ibid., p. 36.

43. Ibid., p. 38.

44. Montessori, Childhood Education, pp. 83-4.

45. Montessori, The Child in the Church, p. 141.

46. Montessori, Childhood Education, pp. 21-2

47. Ibid, p. 83.

48. Montessori, The Secret of Childhood, p. 46.

49. Ibid.

50. Montessori, Childhood Education, p. 13.

CHAPTER III THE CONCEPT OF EDUCATION AND ITS RELATION TO PERSONALITY AND CHARACTER

51. Montessori, Education and Peace, pp. 122-4

52. Montessori, The Child in the Church, p. 141.

53. Montessori, The Secret of Childhood, p. 51.

54. Montessori, Spontaneous Activity in Education, p. 70.

55. Montessori, Spontaneous Activity in Education, p. 70.

56. Ibid., p. 113.

57. Montessori, Absorbent Mind, p. 203.

58. Montessori, Spontaneous Activity in Education, p. 71.

59. For an indepth analysis of Montessori's concept of liberty consult Hanspaul Hager, The Concept of Liberty and the Delineation of Authority as Found in the Writings of Dr. Maria Montessori, a research paper reprinted by the American Montessori Society, 1971, Vol. 9, No. 1.

60. Montessori, Spontaneous Activity in Education, p. 169.

61. Ibid., p. 83.

62. Ibid., p. 163.

63. Ibid.

64. Ibid., p. 161

65. Ibid., p. 78.

66. Ibid., p. 72.

67. Ibid., p. 73.

68. Montessori, The Secret of Childhood, p. 118.

69. Montessori, Absorbent Mind, p. 141.

70. Ibid., p. 142.

71. Ibid.

72. Montessori, Spontaneous Activity in Education, pp. 170-1.

73. Ibid., p. 68.

74. Ibid., pp. 174-5.

75. Ibid., p. 153.

76. Ibid.

77. Ibid., p. 154

78. Ibid.

79. Ibid., p. 184.

80. Ibid., p. 157.

81. Ibid., p. 331.

82. Ibid., pp. 340-1. The similarity of Montessori's notion of "voice of conscience" and Plato's Theory of Reminiscence is remarkable. To the degree that an individual of Plato's Utopia was able to develop and educate his mind to that degree was he able to "remember" or recall the existence of the Realm of True Form. Montessori's view of a "voice of conscience" is interestingly similar. To the degree that one is able to "educate" and develop his "mysterious and precious sensibility" to that degree is one able to "feel" or sense that which is naturally good.

83. Ibid., p. 337.

CHAPTER IV SUMMARY AND DISCUSSION

84. William Heard Kilpatrick, The Montessori System Examined (New York: Houghton Mifflin Company, 1914), pp. 8-9.

85. Ibid., pp. 9-10.

86. Ibid., p. 11.

87. Ibid., p. 12.

88. Ibid., pp. 27-9.

89. Ibid., p. 33.

90. Ibid., p. 34.

91. Ibid., p. 41.

92. Ibid., p. 42-43.

93. Ibid., p. 52.

94. Ibid., p. 55.

95. Ibid., p. 56.

96. Ibid., pp. 58-9.

97. Ibid., p. 59.

98. Ibid., p. 66.

99. Ibid., p. 67.

100. David Norbert Campbell, "A Critical Analysis of William Heard Kilpatrick's The Montessori System Examined" (unpublished

Ph.D. dissertation, University of Illinois at
Urbana-Champaign, 1970), p. 25.

101.   Ibid., p. 31.

102.   Ibid., p. 37.

103.   Ibid., pp. 34-5.

104.   Ibid., p. 35.

105.   Ibid., p. 36.

106.   Ibid., pp. 41-2.

107.   Ibid., p. 43.

108   Ibid., p. 45.

109.   Ibid., p. 46.

110.   Ibid., p. 48.

111.   Ibid., p. 49.

112.   Ibid., p. 51.

113.   Ibid., p. 52.

114.   Ibid., p. 56.

115.   Ibid., p. 61.

116.   Ibid.

117.   Ibid., p. 94.

118.   Ibid., p. 104.

119.   Ibid., p. 95.

120. Ibid., p. 96.

121. Ibid., p. 52.

122. Ibid., p. 95.

123. Montessori, Childhood Education, p. 8.

124. Ibid.

125. Montessori, The Child in the Church, p. 141.

BIBLIOGRAPHY

Campbell, David Norbert. "A Critical Analysis of William Heard Kilpatrick's The Montessori System Examined." The unpublished Ph.D. dissertation, University of Illinois at Urbana-Champaign, 1970.

Kilpatrick, William Heard. The Montessori System Examined. New York: Houghton Mifflin Co., 1914.

Montessori, Maria. Absorbent Mind. New York: Holt, Rinehart & Winston, 1967.

_____. "A Centenary Anthology 1870-1970." Koninginneweg, Amsterdam: Association Montessori Internationale, 1970.

_____. The Child. Adyar, India: Theosophical Publishing House, 1941.

_____. The Child in the Church. London: Sands & Co.: St. Louis: B. Herder Book Co., 1929.

_____. Childhood Education. Chicago: Henry Regnery Company, 1974.

_____. Discovery of the Child. Notre Dame: Fides Publishers, Inc., 1967.

_____. Education and Peace. Chicago: Henry Regnery Co., 1972.

_____. Education for a New World. Thiruvanmiyur, Indian: Kalekshetra Publications, 1946.

_____. From Child to Adolescence. New York: Schocken Books, Inc., 1973.

_____. Montessori Elementary Material. New York: Schocken Books, Inc., 1973.

_____. The Montessori Method. New York: Schocken Books, Inc., 1964.

_____. Peace and Education. Adyar, India: Theosophical Publishing House, 1943.

_____. Reconstruction in Education, Adyar, India: Theosophical Publishing House, 1942.

_____. The Secret of Childhood. Notre Dame: Fides Publishers, Inc., 1966.

_____. Spontaneous Activity in Education. New York: Schocken Books, 1965.

_____. What You Should Know About Your Child. Adyar, India: Kalakshetra Publications, 1966.

Standing, E. M. Maria Montessori: Her Life and Works. New York and London: New American Library, Inc., 1962.